STUMP KINGDOM

STUMP KINGDOM

ISAIAH 6-12

DALE RALPH DAVIS

CHRISTIAN
FOCUS

All Scriputre quotations are the author's own translation.

ISBN Nos:
paperback 978-1-5271-0006-0
epub 978-1-5271-0037-4
mobi 978-1-5271-0038-1

Published in 2017
by
Christian Focus Publications Ltd,
Geanies House, Fearn, Ross-shire,
IV20 1TW, Scotland, UK.

www.christianfocus.com

Cover design by Daniel van Straaten

Printed by Bell & Bain, Glasgow

Contents

Abbreviations

ABD	*Anchor Bible Dictionary*
DCH	*Dictionary of Classical Hebrew* (ed. D. J. A. Clines)
ESV	English Standard Version
ISBE	*International Standard Bible Encyclopedia*
KJV	King James (Authorized) Version
K-B	Koehler & Baumgartner, *Hebrew and Aramaic Lexicon*
NBD	*New Bible Dictionary*
NIDOTTE	*New International Dictionary of Old Testament Theology and Exegesis*
NIV	New International Version
NKJV	New King James Version
RSV	Revised Standard Version
TDOT	*Theological Dictionary of the Old Testament*

Preface

There is no special reason for producing this treatment of Isaiah 6–12, except that I wanted to work through the text again for myself. I especially wanted to deal with Isaiah 7, for I am convinced there is no need to stoop to any 'double fulfillment' shenanigans there. I have tried to keep the exposition semi-popular, but it was necessary to wade through more detail in Isaiah 7.

Christ's people have been put in immense debt in recent years with top-flight commentaries on Isaiah, especially the battery of two-volume ones by John L. MacKay, John Oswalt, Gary V. Smith, and Alec Motyer (Dr Motyer's are not 'matching' ones, but a 'big' one in 1993 and a smaller 'Tyndale' one in 1999 – but they are by no means duplicates). My debt to these and others is evident repeatedly.

I am the 'caboose' of a family of five boys, hence I have had four older brothers, whose deeds and tales of them have been the stuff of truth and legend in our family over the years. So it is simply appropriate that I send forth this brief study as a tribute to Walt, Glenn, and Jim – and in memory of Red.

DALE RALPH DAVIS
Autumn 2016

1 KNOCKED OUT OF YOUR SENSES
(Isaiah 6:1-13)

(1) In the year of King Uzziah's death I saw the Lord, sitting upon a throne, high and lifted up, and the trails of his robe were filling the temple.

(2) Seraphs were standing above him. Each one had six wings. With two he would cover his face, and with two he would cover his feet, and with two he would fly.

(3) And this one called out to that one and said, 'Holy, holy, holy is Yahweh of hosts – his glory is what fills all the earth.'

(4) Then the foundations of the thresholds shook because of the voice of the one who called out – and the house was filled with smoke.

(5)   And I said, 'Woe to me! For I am destroyed! For I am a man of unclean lips, and I dwell in the midst of a people of unclean lips; indeed my eyes have seen **the king**, Yahweh of hosts.'

(6)   Then one of the seraphs flew to me and in his hand was a glowing coal – he had taken it with tongs from the altar.

(7)   And he let it touch my mouth and said: 'See! This has touched your lips – and your guilt has been taken away and your sin will be covered.'

(8)   Then I heard the Lord's voice, saying, 'Whom should I send, and who will go for us?' And I said, 'Here I am – send me.'

(9)   And he said,

'Go, and you shall say to this people,
"Go on hearing, and do not understand,
go on seeing, and do not come to perceive;"

(10) *make the heart of this people fat,*
and make their ears heavy,
and make their eyes blind,
lest they should see with their eyes,
and hear with their ears,
and understand with their hearts
– and turn and get healed!'

(11) So I said, 'How long, O Lord?' And he said, 'Until cities crash into ruins without any residents, and houses contain no people, and the ground is ruined – a devastation;

(12) and Yahweh shall remove people far off, and the forsaken place is huge in the midst of the land;

(13) and when there is yet a tenth in it – it too will experience burning; like the terebinth and like the oak, which, when felled, their stump remains – the holy seed is its stump'.

Privileges are not all they're cracked up to be. On a Sunday in April in 1865, in a remote hamlet called Appomattox Courthouse (Virginia), the parlor of one Wilmer McLean was selected for Generals Lee and Grant to confer over the surrender of Lee's Confederate army to Grant and the Federals. By 4:00 p.m. all was over but the pillaging. One Federal officer 'bought' the table on which the surrender terms were drafted, another the table on which the terms were signed; some officers carried off chairs, while others cut the seats out of cane-bottom chairs and handed out strips of cane as souvenirs to Federal officers outside. Alas, there's a price for making history – your house can be ransacked![1]

It is something like that with 'seeing the Lord' in Isaiah 6. One can simply be glad it was Isaiah. That way we can read about it and watch – hopefully – at a distance. Isaiah's report of his call is very sense-oriented; he focuses on what he sees, feels, and hears. But the privilege of the vision Isaiah has (v. 1) brings him smack up against the terror of God's holiness. If Isaiah says, 'I saw the Lord' (v. 1), he also has to say, 'I am destroyed' (v. 5). We'll try to unpack Isaiah's vision by tracing what he sees, feels, and hears.

So note, first of all, **what he sees – a dreadful God** (vv. 1-5). In his vision Isaiah sees the Lord and hears the seraphs' song. He hears *the big word: holy.* 'Holy, holy, holy is Yahweh of hosts – his glory is what fills all the earth' (v. 3). Holiness is the massive fact about God. Let's see if we can't scrape together an idea of what holy/holiness is primarily from the confines of this passage.

The text suggests that holiness is something *extra-ordinary.* You may be tempted to say that's obvious; but look at the way the text depicts this. One assumes that seraphs attending Yahweh's presence must be sinless beings, but even sinless seraphs cover

---

1. Burke Davis, *The Civil War: Strange and Fascinating Facts* (New York: Fairfax, 1982), pp. 20-21. The irony is that McLean had moved to Appomattox to get away from the war; in 1861 he had been living near Bull Run!

face and feet (v. 2b). So holiness is not mere sinlessness – It is beyond that. One thinks of that stanza in Matthew Bridges' hymn: 'No angel in the sky / can fully bear that sight / but downward bends his burning eye / at mysteries so bright.' Here A. W. Tozer's counsel is apt:

> We cannot grasp the true meaning of the divine holiness by thinking of someone or something very pure and then raising the concept to the highest degree we are capable of. God's holiness is not simply the best we know infinitely bettered. We know nothing like the divine holiness. It stands apart, unique, unapproachable, incomprehensible and unattainable. The natural man is blind to it. He may fear God's power and admire his wisdom, but his holiness he cannot even imagine.[2]

And it is even beyond seraphs. They speak of it but shield themselves from it.

Let us stick with the seraphs and note that holiness is something *thrilling*. 'This one called out to that one and said, "Holy, holy, holy is Yahweh of hosts...."' (v. 3). The three-fold repetition suggests the intensity (or density?) of Yahweh's holiness. Repetition is the way Bible writers indicate bold print or upper-case letters or exclamation marks. One finds triple repetition in a negative sense in Ezekiel 21:27 ('A ruin, ruin, ruin I will make it'). There Yahweh speaks of the complete devastation of the kingdom of Judah under Zedekiah. It will be nothing but ruin, utter and total ruin. Ruin in *excelsis*. Here the repetition is used 'positively'. But there is something we can miss. These repeated cries of the seraphs are a kind of back-and-forth *praise*, indicating that they find this proclamation of Yahweh's holiness delightful – and they are entering into it with gusto. And the repetition shows their excitement and enthusiasm over his holiness – it thrills them

---

2. A. W. Tozer, *The Knowledge of the Holy* (New York: Harper & Row, 1961), p. 111.

to the bottom of their burning beings. May the contagion infect us!

The seraphs also tell us that holiness is something *aggressive*: 'his glory is what fills all the earth' (v. 3b). 'Glory' is what holiness is like when it's visible; 'glory' is holiness with a wrapper around it. And this glory either does (if the text implies present time) or is going to (if future) fill the whole earth. God's holiness is going to take over. Holiness is not some tame, docile, dormant, reclusive quality in God – it is going to go on display throughout the earth (Hab. 2:14).

And then Isaiah's response tells us that holiness is something *alarming*: 'Woe to me! For I am destroyed! For I am a man of unclean lips' (v. 5). Holiness is frightening, because the prophet is the opposite of what Yahweh is – he is 'unclean.' Here he does not mean unclean in simply a ritual or technical sense; rather he uses the term in a 'moral' sense, and by the contrast indicates that there is a moral purity or perfection in God's holiness. Isaiah's response is very like that of the men of Beth-shemesh as they gazed on a God-sent local disaster: 'Who is able to stand before Yahweh, this holy God?' (1 Sam. 6:20). Perhaps in light of verses 1-5 we could say that holiness is something like the awe-inspiring majesty of the godness of God.[3]

That is the big word – holy. Now we hear *the sad truth* – 'I am destroyed!' (v. 5). Isaiah is alarmed because of his lips and his eyes: 'I am a man of unclean lips' and 'my eyes have seen the king.' Why does he focus on lips? Well, if he is called to proclaim Yahweh's word, how can he do that with defiled lips? It would be like someone wanting to be an auto mechanic when he had had both arms amputated. But likely there's more. How can the prophet even join in the praises of the seraphs

---

3. cf. Raymond C. Ortlund, Jr. (*Isaiah: God Saves Sinners* [Wheaton: Crossway, 2005], p. 77): 'His holiness is simply his God-ness in all his attributes, works, and ways.'

with unclean lips? So his defilement hinders both his vocation and his worship. Clearly, Isaiah did not think this was 'just the neatest experience' but the most dreadful moment of his life.

What is the overflow here for Joe or Jane Christian? Well, we might say that we have here a sample of one of God's finest gifts. For this point it doesn't matter whether you think chapter 6 is Isaiah's 're-commissioning' after he had begun to prophesy (chapters 1–5) or whether you think chapter 6 is the prophet's original call placed for particular reasons after a collection of his preaching (chapters 1–5). Whatever the case, Isaiah was already a believer when he had this vision; he was not a pagan; in our lingo this is a post-conversion experience. And this is one of God's best gifts to you as a Christian: to give you an overpowering and increasing sense of how total and filthy your corruption is, of how deeply tangled and devious you are.

Dr John 'Rabbi' Duncan (d. 1870) didn't seem to have any vision like Isaiah and yet came to the same realization. One Sabbath evening he was cogitating on his more than seventy years of life and broke out in a soliloquy:

> There are heaps o' things in the past, mercies, sins, forgivenesses; in seventy years and better there is a great deal to look back to. Alas! I have never done a sinless action during it all; I have never done a sinless action during the seventy years. I don't say but by God's grace there may have been some holy action done, but never a sinless action during the seventy years. What an awful thing is human life! and what a solemn consideration it should be to us, that we have never done a sinless action all our life, that we have never done one act that did not need to be pardoned.[4]

That's very Isaiah-like. And it came after this eccentric Scottish minister and academic had served his Lord for a life-time. He was a man of unclean lips.

---

4. A. Moody Stuart, *The Life of John Duncan* (orig. pub. 1872; Edinburgh: Banner of Truth, 1991), p. 150.

Or think of John Murray, for many years the professor of theology at Westminster Seminary in Philadelphia. Murray was, with several others, enjoying the hospitality of Pastor and Mrs Freeman in their home. They had all been discussing the innate sinfulness of the human heart and Murray himself had been speaking of the depth of human depravity. Then Mrs Freeman interjected, 'But Mr Murray, we know that you are not as bad as that.' Now my hunch is that Professor Murray may have 'missed' something at that point. I don't know, but it sounds like Mrs Freeman might have been kidding him and he simply didn't catch the sparkle in her eye or the lilt in her voice. In any case, he fixed his good eye on her and said sternly: 'Mrs Freeman, if you knew what a cesspool of iniquity this vile heart of mine is you would never say such a thing!'[5] As if he had said, 'I am a man of unclean lips – and much, much more!'

What has all this to do with service to Christ? Simply that God always begins with the servant. And whether you are serving with a mission in Kenya or serving by teaching school in Dingwall, you must begin with your own unclean lips or you won't be fit to serve anywhere.

Secondly, Isaiah depicts **what he feels – a painful purging** (vv. 6-7). Here is the response to the prophet's cry in verse 5. 'Then one of the seraphs flew to me, and in his hand was a glowing coal – he had taken it with tongs from the altar' (v. 6). Note the source of the glowing coal: it came from the 'altar.' Contrary to many expositors, I think the 'altar' intended is a counterpart (remember it's a vision) to the altar of burnt offering in the temple courts. On the Day of Atonement the high priest got coals for incense from the altar of burnt offering

---

5. Iain H. Murray, *Life of John Murray*, in *Collected Writings of John Murray*, vol. 3: *Life of John Murray, Sermons & Reviews* (Edinburgh: Banner of Truth, 1982), p. 76.

and then took them into the Holy Place (Lev. 16:12).[6] Some may say that imagery in a vision can be rather fluid and we should not try to be too precise. But the point is rather important: the coal comes from the place of sacrifice, the place where a substitute was offered for the people's sins. The antidote for Isaiah's danger and defilement comes from the God-provided place of atonement.

And don't you wince at the pain? 'He let it touch my mouth' (v. 7a). I know, it's 'only' a vision, you might say. But we can get caught up in the drama of a play or a movie when it's only a play or a movie. Don't you cringe then as you envision the scene, as you watch that glowing coal singe his lips? But the meaning of this act is more important than the pain. The seraph does not leave Isaiah in the dark; this is not a charade he must figure out but an action that is interpreted for him. 'See! This has touched your lips – and your guilt has been taken away and your sin will be covered' (v. 7b). What had taken place on the altar was applied to Isaiah's need; this atonement lifted both the load of his guilt and the offense of his deeds.

If you are what is sometimes called a 'New Testament believer', don't think this matter does not apply to you, for, as Hebrews 13:10 assures us, 'We have an altar,' a place where a substitute was offered, where one was destroyed in your place. That altar, as the following context makes clear, is the cross of Jesus outside Jerusalem. That is where your guilt is taken away and your sin covered.

What is so delightful about this segment of Isaiah's vision is that it shows that the God who makes you see your filthiness

---

6. See Baruch A. Levine, *Leviticus*, The JPS Torah Commentary (Philadelphia: Jewish Publication Society, 1989), p. 104; Jacob Milgrom, *Leviticus 1-16*, The Anchor Bible (New York: Doubleday, 1991), p. 1025; and G. J. Wenham, *The Book of Leviticus*, New International Commentary on the Old Testament (Grand Rapids: Eerdmans, 1979), p. 231. There was a continual fire on the altar of burnt offering (Lev. 6:12-13).

has also provided for your cleansing – all of which is based on an atoning sacrifice. We may be too jaded over this, almost too accustomed to hearing this that it has ceased to 'grab' us. Have you ever thought what life would be like *without atonement*?

In one of my previous books I told of Admiral Onishi, who tried to provide his own atonement. Takijiro Onishi was Commander of Japan's First Air Fleet. It was October 1944 and the war was turning sour for Japan in the Pacific. Onishi therefore proposed desperate measures. 'In my opinion,' he said, 'the enemy can be stopped only by crash-diving on their carrier flight decks with Zero fighters carrying 250-kilogram bombs.' Hence kamikaze pilots, suicide attacks. Onishi was adamant: 'Nothing short of all-out use of special attacks can save us.' Such suicide attacks were much more successful than conventional air strikes. By the time Japan surrendered in August 1945, 2,519 men and officers of the Imperial Japanese Navy had sacrificed themselves. On the evening of August 15, Admiral Onishi left a note: 'To the souls of my late subordinates I express the greatest appreciation for their valiant deeds. In death I wish to apologize to these brave men and their families.' He then plunged a samurai sword into his mid-section. He refused medical attention, would permit no one to finish him off. He lingered in agony until six o'clock the following evening. The tellers of his story conclude by saying: 'His choice to endure prolonged suffering was obviously made in expiation for his part in one of the most diabolical tactics of war the world has ever seen.'[7] But there is no atonement there – on the bloody blade of a samurai sword. The self-appointed gore of my intestines cannot dissolve my guilt. Only when I receive that cauterizing coal from Yahweh's 'Jerusalem altar'

---

7. Rikihei Inoguchi and Tadashi Nakajima, ' Death on the Wing,' *Secrets and Spies: Behind-the-Scenes Stories of World War II* (Pleasantville, NY: Reader's Digest Association, 1964), p. 447-51.

do I ever hear 'your guilt has been taken away and your sin will be covered.' Then you do not have to worship the Lord in the *terror* of holiness but in the *safety* of holiness.

In the third place, Isaiah relates **what he hears – a devastating message** (vv. 8-13). Isaiah hears the Lord's call, we could say his invitation (v. 8a), and he volunteers (v. 8b) to go in Yahweh's name. And then one meets a real 'downer' (vv. 9-13). Well, not all is bleak – there would be a 'stump' people (v. 13c), a remnant we would say, for Jesus will never allow his people to be eradicated. But, on the whole, these verses are not a delightful, optimistic beginning to a prophetic vocation.

In broad terms we can detect two keynotes in this section. One is the problem of preaching (vv. 9-10). Let me try to summarize what Yahweh tells Isaiah here: On the whole they won't listen (v. 9); in fact, your preaching will have a deadening, densifying, deafening impact on them; they will become so immune to it that they cannot respond and this is my judgment on them (v. 10).[8]

The second keynote is the honesty of God (vv. 11-13a) – and I want you to see that this is relatively encouraging. Isaiah's 'How long?' probably does not refer to how long he must go on preaching in this way but to how long this hardness of heart is going to be the case in Judah. Yahweh's answer is: until and through the time when the land is ruined and the people taken captive and even what's left gets wiped out again (vv. 11b-13a). This is a devastating message! Yet I want you to see that there is *a certain kindness* in the way God deals with his servant – and there is a spillover for any Christian. It's as if Yahweh says, 'What you do, Isaiah, will not be very successful – in fact, it

---

8. 'The truth that God hardens the hearts of sinners is taught frequently in the Scriptures (Rom. 9:18; 2 Thess. 2:11). But it is equally important to bear in mind that the hearts that he hardens are not morally neutral, but corrupt and sinful' (Derek Thomas, *God Delivers: Isaiah Simply Explained* [Darlington: Evangelical Press, 1991], p. 67).

will be apparently fruitless.' Isaiah then was to labor under no illusions; if he has little success, he need not despair of his call or think there is some gross inadequacy in his ministry. Isn't God good then to be so up-front with Isaiah? He will have no misconceptions about what he will meet. In principle it reminds me of what Jonathan Edwards told Elihu Parsons when he asked for the hand of Edwards' daughter Sally in marriage. Edwards told him plainly of her 'unpleasant temper'. Parsons persisted with 'But she has grace, I trust?' (i.e., she is converted after all, isn't she?) Edwards retorted, 'I hope she has, but grace can live where you cannot.'[9] As if to say, 'Do you realize what a hornets' nest you'd be walking into? I'm sure I wouldn't want to deal with that nasty temper day after day.' Not exactly a complimentary thing to say about one's daughter, but, from another angle, a very kind and gracious warning to Mr Parsons.

That's why Isaiah can trust his Lord: he hides nothing from him; he tells him exactly how tough it will be. And that should – perhaps in a back-handed way – hearten us as well.

I say this because sometimes our Christian sub-culture gives the impression that if you have enough faith, if you practice biblical principles of relationships, if you bathe your activities in prayer, if you formulate a creative ministry strategy, if you devise a workable vision statement, if you attend the latest how-to conferences, subscribe to certain Christian magazines or listen to particular Christian blogs – well then, you cannot help but have success in Christian service or ministry. Really? I don't know if Jesus swallowed that. He told his disciples some pretty tough stuff (John 15:18-27) and then said, 'These things I have spoken to you so that you may be kept from stumbling' (John 16:1, NASB). Isn't God so very good to tell you how very

---

9. Iain H. Murray, *Jonathan Edwards: A New Biography* (Edinburgh: Banner of Truth, 1987), p. 192.

nasty and difficult and cruddy it may be? Can't you trust a truthful God like that, who does not give you 'bum steers' about the service he calls you to do?

Now I haven't said anything about King Uzziah who died in verse 1. Uzziah reigned a total of fifty-two years (2 Kings 15:2; 2 Chron. 26:3), and such continuity gave the people of Judah a great deal of stability. Now he's gone. But the Lord is still reigning: 'In the year of King Uzziah's death I saw the Lord, *sitting upon a throne.*' You may need to hear that and to remember that he is the holy God who knocks you right out of your senses, for here you see and feel and hear that the holy God is a frightening God, that the holy God is an atoning God, that the holy God is a candid God – the sort of God who makes you want to say, 'Here I am – send me.'

THE BAD NEWS AND GOOD NEWS OF IMMANUEL
(Isaiah 7:1–8:10)

(1)   Now in the days of Ahaz, son of Jotham, king of Judah, Rezin, king of Aram, went up, along with Pekah, son of Remaliah, king of Israel – they went up to Jerusalem to make war against it, but they were not successful in fighting against it.

(2)   And it was told to the house of David, 'Aram has settled down with Ephraim,' and his heart and the heart of his people trembled like the trees of the forest tremble because of the wind.

(3)   Then Yahweh said to Isaiah, 'Go out now to meet Ahaz, you and Shear-jashub, your son, to the end of the conduit of the upper pool, to the highway to the Fuller's Field.

(4) And you shall say to him, "Watch out and remain quiet; do not be afraid and do not let your heart be fearful because of these two smoking stumps of firebrands, at the hot anger of Rezin and Aram and of the son of Remaliah.

(5) Because Aram has planned disaster against you, (along with) Ephraim and the son of Remaliah, saying,

(6) 'Let us go up against Judah and let us tear it up and break it open for ourselves and install as king in the midst of it the son of Tabal,'

(7) – here's what the Lord Yahweh says, "It will not hold up and it will not come about,

(8) for the head of Aram is Damascus and the head of Damascus is Rezin – and within sixty-five years Ephraim will be so shattered he will not be a people,

(9) and the head of Ephraim is Samaria and the head of Samaria the son of Remaliah; if you will not remain firm, you will not be made firm."'

(10) Then Yahweh again spoke to Ahaz:

(11) 'Ask for yourself a sign from Yahweh your God;
      make it deep as Sheol or high as the height above.'

(12) And Ahaz said,
      'I will not ask, and I will not put Yahweh to the test.'

(13) So he said,
      'Listen now, house of David,
      Is it too small a matter that you weary men
      that you will weary even my God?

(14) Therefore, the Lord himself will give you a sign:
      See! A virgin, pregnant, and going to give birth to a
          son,
      and she shall call his name Immanuel.

(15) Curds and honey he will eat

so that he may know rejecting evil and choosing
good;

(16)   to be sure, before the lad knows rejecting evil and
choosing good
the ground which you are tearing up will be forsaken
of both its kings.

(17)   Yahweh will bring upon you
and upon your people and upon your father's house
days which have never come
from the day Ephraim departed from Judah
– the king of Assyria.'

(18) And it shall be on that day
Yahweh will whistle
for the fly which is at the end of the Nile-canals of
Egypt
and for the bee which is in the land of Assyria,

(19) and they shall come and settle down
– all of them –
in the deep-cut wadis
and in the clefts of the rocks
and on all the thornbushes
and all the watering-holes.

(20) On that day the Lord will shave
with a rented razor
from beyond the River,
with the king of Assyria,
the head and the hair of the legs
and it will sweep away even the beard.

(21) And it shall be on that day
a man will keep alive a heifer from the herd
and a couple of sheep,

(22) and it shall be
because of the plenteous milk they produce

23

he will eat curds,
for one will eat curds and honey
– everyone who is left within the land.

(23) And it shall be on that day
every place where there used to be
  a thousand vines worth a thousand silver-weight
will become thornbushes
and will become briers.

(24) With arrows and bow one will go in there,
for all the land will be thornbushes and briers,

(25) and all the hills that used to be hoed with a hoe
– you won't go there
for fear of thornbushes and briers,
and it shall be a place for the ox to go loose
and for the sheep to trample (Isa. 7:1-25).

(1) Then Yahweh said to me, 'Get yourself a large tablet and write on it with an ordinary (?) stylus, "Belonging to Rush-to-plunder-speed-to-spoil."'

(2) And I got myself reliable witnesses – Uriah the priest and Zechariah the son of Jeberechiah.

(3) Then I came near the prophetess and she became pregnant and gave birth to a son; and Yahweh said to me, 'Call his name Rush-to-plunder-speed-to-spoil,

(4) for before the lad knows to call out "My father" or "My mother," the wealth of Damascus and the plunder of Samaria will be carried off before the king of Assyria.'

(5) Then Yahweh spoke to me again, saying,

(6) 'Because this people have rejected the waters of Shiloah that flow along gently and exult [about] Rezin and the son of Remaliah,

(7) and therefore – see! – the Lord is bringing up against them the mighty and many waters of the River, the king

of Assyria and all his glory, and he shall go up over all his channels and overflow all his banks,

(8) and he shall sweep on into Judah; he shall overflow and rush on; he will reach right up to the neck; and the outstretching of his wings shall fill the breadth of your land, O Immanuel.'

(9) Do your worst, O peoples,
   and be shattered;
   and listen, all distant places of the earth:
       Get yourselves ready and be shattered!
       Get yourselves ready and be shattered!

(10) Hatch a plan – and it will be frustrated;
    speak a word – and it will never stand,
    for … Immanuel! (Isa. 8:1-10).

It was early in the 1920 baseball season. Fire-baller Walter Johnson was pitching for Washington against the Cleveland Indians. The Cleveland shortstop was batting and Johnson quickly blew two blazing strikes past him. The batter turned away and walked toward the dugout. The umpire hollered after him that he only had two strikes. Back came the answer: 'I know it. You can have the next one.' It didn't matter. Walter Johnson would strike him out anyway. There was no use hanging around to experience it.

Dealing with the Immanuel prophecy can be a good bit like facing Walter Johnson. It seems a nearly hopeless task. One has to wade through numerous textual debates and interpretive questions, all of which tempt one to 'walk back to the dugout'. But there are some studies that provide substantial help and so it seems worthwhile to risk an extended exposition of the text, disputed as it is.[1] I mean to cover, after a fashion, all of

---

1. Especially helpful is J. Barton Payne, 'Right Questions about Isaiah 7:14,' in *The Living and Active Word of God: Studies in Honor of Samuel J.*

7:1–8:10, but my focus will always be on 'the prophecy', by which I mean 7:14 (in its context):

> Therefore, the Lord himself will give you a sign: See! A virgin, pregnant, and going to give birth to a son, and she shall call his name Immanuel.

So let us plunge in. The first discovery we make is that Immanuel is bad news.

The setting of this prophecy: the judgment on unbelief (7:1-17)

Background to the prophecy (vv. 1-9)

It was 734 B.C. and the sun was not shining outside the conference room in Jerusalem where King Ahaz was huddling with his foreign policy wonks. Judah was caving in. Syria had driven the men of Judah out of Elath, the seaport on the Gulf of Aqabah (2 Kings 16:6) – a huge economic and commercial loss for Judah. This likely meant that Judah had also lost any control she had of the King's Highway, the prime north-south trade route east of the Jordan. Edomites to the southeast were invading; Philistines from the west had pilfered territory and towns (2 Chron. 28:17-18); Syria and Israel were inflicting staggering losses in war (2 Chron. 28:5-8). And now Syria and Israel, united in what historians dub 'the Syro-Ephraimite Alliance,' were threatening to overrun Jerusalem and install their own puppet king on the throne of David/Ahaz (back to Isa. 7:6). The usual 'take' on this scenario holds that Syria and Israel were

---

Schultz, ed. Morris Inch and Ronald Youngblood (Winona Lake, IN: Eisenbrauns, 1983), pp. 75-84. I did not happen on to Payne's article until fairly recently. I had reached some similar conclusions as he and then discovered he had already reached them! Which is both heartening and humbling. Much earlier I had also found Alec Motyer's article immensely helpful: 'Context and Content in the Interpretation of Isaiah 7:14,' *Tyndale Bulletin* 21 (1970), pp. 118-25.

wanting to form an anti-Assyrian coalition in the west (to hold off Assyria's dominance there) and Ahaz had refused to join the 'Allies' – hence Rezin of Syria and Pekah of Israel decided to usher Ahaz & Co. into historical limbo and install a 'pliable' lackey in his place.[2] So ... you are in the conference room and you have few options left, few buttons to push. But there is still the panic button, and Ahaz's finger is on it.

But why should we care about what happens to Ahaz? Because Yahweh's reputation is at stake. The shadow of 2 Samuel 7 hovers over Isaiah 7. At the very heart of Isaiah 7 is 2 Samuel 7 and Yahweh's promise to David: 'Your house and your kingdom shall be made sure forever before me; your throne shall be established forever' (2 Sam. 7:16). And the end-product of that line of kings will be a just Ruler (2 Sam. 23:3), namely, the Messiah. So a 'ridiculous' thing happened one day. Who can understand the wild commitments God makes? Yahweh made a promise to David and the whole structure and flow and hope of world history will rest on the existence of a line of kings in a puny Near Eastern state no larger than Connecticut and Rhode Island combined. But if Ahaz and the dynasty of David go down the tube, that is, if these two tinhorn hotheads from north of the border have their way (v. 6), then God's covenant promise to David proves false. No small stakes.

Ahaz and his cronies had severe angst over this anticipated onslaught (v. 2). On one gloomy Thursday or thereabouts, Ahaz was inspecting the Emergency Water Supply System (v. 3) and Isaiah meets up with him to deliver a word of encouragement.

We should also note that walking along beside Isaiah was a 'message in the flesh', a walking sacrament, Isaiah's son Shear-jashub (v. 3).[3] Shear-jashub's name means 'A remnant will

---

2. For a lucid summary and reconstruction, see M. F. Unger, *Israel and the Aramaeans of Damascus* (1957; reprint ed., Grand Rapids: Baker, 1980), pp. 95-101.

3. Some think Shear-jashub's presence here is not particularly significant

return'. He is therefore both assurance and threat to Ahaz & Co. Assurance, in that his name indicates that – let Judah's enemies do their worst – they will never be able to annihilate Judah. A remnant *will return* – Yahweh will always, no matter what, have a people to serve him on this earth. Yet Shear-jashub's name also implied that '*only* a remnant will return', and so it was a threat and a potential word of judgment for the majority of the people of Judah.

Isaiah's message calls Ahaz to trust Yahweh: 'Watch out and remain quiet; do not be afraid and do not let your heart be fearful' (v. 4). As for the scheme of Rezin and Pekah, 'It will not hold up and it will not come about' (v. 7). Rezin may be over Damascus and Pekah (actually, 'the son of Remaliah') over Samaria, but that's all they'll control (vv. 8-9a); they won't control Jerusalem.[4] This word is sure whether or not Ahaz believes, but, in fact, Ahaz *is* called upon to believe Yahweh's promise of protection: 'If you will not remain firm, you will not be made firm' (v. 9b). There's a word-play on the Hebrew verb *'āman* (be firm, reliable). And since the verbs in 9b are second person *plural*, it means that both Ahaz and his whole 'administration' are called to lean on Yahweh's promise. The real crisis is not the Syro-Ephraimite threat but the word of Yahweh – and faith or unbelief toward it. Verse 9b does not say, 'If you don't believe, my word will fall'; but it says, 'If you do not believe, *you* will fall, while my word will stand.' The bus will run from Chattanooga to Atlanta no matter what; but if

---

since the text does not seem to draw much attention to him. But must Scripture always fall all over itself and say, 'Hey, this is significant!' in order for something to be significant?

4. Here I follow E. J. Young, *The Book of Isaiah,* 3 vols., The New International Commentary on the Old Testament (Grand Rapids: Eerdmans, 1965), 1:274, 276. The parenthetical note in 8b about Ephraim's '65 years' may refer to Esarhaddon's deportation and resettlement activities in 671 B.C.; cf. 2 Kings 17:24 and Ezra 4:2.

you don't show up, you won't be on it. Isaiah was calling Ahaz & Co. to show up in faith, to trust Yahweh's word of assurance. 'Only trust him.'

Tone of the prophecy (vv. 10-17)
In verses 10-11 Yahweh offers Ahaz a 'sign' that his word of verses 7-9 is true. Yahweh will give Ahaz a visible token, a 'sacrament', to convince Ahaz about how reliable Yahweh's promise is. Ahaz can ask for anything from the sky to the grave and Yahweh will do it. God will do anything to help Ahaz trust him. Ahaz's response (v. 12) is a refusal of the offer of a sign. He sounds pious but it's all humbug. He had already appealed (or was about to appeal) to Tiglath-pileser of Assyria for relief (see 2 Kings 16:7). Who needs Yahweh's word when you can go through a little nose-scraping and boot-licking and bribe Assyria for a sure thing?

Isaiah's exasperated reaction in verse 13 confirms that Ahaz's words in verse 12 were essentially unbelief. This means that the introductory 'Therefore' in verse 14a introduces a *threat*, a *judgment-word* on Ahaz & Co. (Hebrew *lākēn* [law-cane], 'therefore,' often introduces an expression of judgment; see, e.g., 1:24; 5:13, 14, 24; and Amos 4:12). Instead of a sign *offered* (v. 11), there will be a sign *imposed* (v. 14). The sign is: 'See! A virgin, pregnant, and going to give birth to a son; and she shall call his name Immanuel.'

The whole of verses 14-17 is a word of judgment – yes, even of defiance – to Ahaz and his cronies. The overall thrust of these verses is: The dynasty of David is going to continue – anyway. A virgin of all things (or people) is going to conceive a son, an amazing feat, and his name will be called Immanuel – hence this Descendant of David will be no ordinary king. Note the *conditions* under which this Immanuel-child will exist (v. 15). He'll eat 'curds and honey', which, according to verse 22, is the diet of a people and land devastated and at poverty level. (Curds and honey are *not* the food of paradise, as some have alleged; people who eat yogurt and cottage cheese are *not* having the time of their lives.) This Immanuel, then, will not come on the scene until Judah goes through the darkest of times, ravaged by war (vv. 20-25; these verses explain the curds-and-honey level of existence noted in v. 15). And who is it who will bring this devastation and ruin on Judah? Not Rezin or Pekah but the king of Assyria (v. 17), the very 'savior' in whom Ahaz had placed his trust. And verses 18-25 spell out in detail, as if in a set of four photo-slides (vv. 18-19, 20, 21-22, 23-25), what the Assyrian desolation will be like.

Take in, then, the overall flow of the prophecy: Immanuel is *bad news* for Ahaz. The king Ahaz will receive will *not* be Immanuel but the king of Assyria (v. 17). This Immanuel figure apparently won't come on the scene until after Judah goes through the darkest of times, ruin by Assyria – something for which they can thank Ahaz and his suave foreign policy. Immanuel is someone in whom Ahaz *has no part*; he is *removed from* Ahaz. Ahaz has chosen the king of Assyria and he will get him (v. 17) – to his detriment (2 Chron. 28:20). But he will not have 'God with us'. In Ahaz's unbelief, one could almost say, the house of David has rejected the covenant with David.

One hesitates to keep hammering on this. But I feel a bit like that motel-chain owner who was asked what he would want to tell his customers if he could only say one thing to them. He responded: 'The shower curtain goes on the *inside* of the tub!' One may be surprised that such words would constitute his premier message, but apparently his motels had suffered a good bit of water damage from patrons' carelessness.

So let me come at you again. You *must* hear the judgment tone of verses 10-17 in their *context*. The king whose name is 'God with us' will only come after Ahaz has brought ruin on the nation. As Peter said to Simon in reference to the gift of the Holy Spirit, so Isaiah seems to say to Ahaz in reference to Immanuel: 'You have neither part nor lot in this matter' (Acts 8:21, RSV). All this must be kept in mind when many claim that the child promised in verse 14 must have been one who was somehow contemporary with Ahaz, in order for the prophecy to have some relevance to Ahaz. But that is just Isaiah's point: *Immanuel has no relevance to Ahaz.* Ahaz has chosen the king of Assyria instead. But Immanuel *will* come in spite of Ahaz and his unbelief – but he will not come for Ahaz. This means we should quit looking for a 'contemporary fulfillment' in Ahaz's own time. There is none.[5]

Details of the prophecy

Now I want to discuss bits and pieces of the text in verses 14-17, for how one understands the import of these details shapes the way one understands the thrust of the prophecy as a whole.

1. The 'virgin'/*'almah* in verse 14. The term is rather rare (seven times really) and not every use gives help toward determining meaning. The word occurs in Genesis 24:43 of the unmarried Rebekah; earlier (24:16) we'd been told that no man had had sexual relations with her. Moses' sister is an *'almah* (Exod. 2:8), and it may be she had not even reached double-digit age. The plural is used in Song of Songs 6:8, where the *'alamôth* stand over against sixty queens and eighty concubines and so would be unmarried and presumably virgins. Based on scanty usage one could say that an *'almah* is a young girl or woman, as yet unmarried, though she may be of marriageable age. The term probably does not convey the idea of virginity by definition but by assumption, i.e., in

---

5. Some may question how verse 14 could be a 'sign' for Ahaz if it were not contemporary with him, if it would come about beyond Ahaz's time. But the sign was not for Ahaz individually, or perhaps even primarily – it was for 'the house of David' (v. 13), which may well include the ongoing Davidic dynasty.

Israelite society, if a young girl might be of marriageable age but not yet married, one would assume – other things being equal – that she was in fact a virgin.

Sometimes one hears the claim that if Isaiah had really intended to say 'virgin', he would have used *betûlah*. But this won't wash. The word occurs fifty-one times in the Old Testament. But if someone wanted to make absolutely clear that a *betûlah* was in fact a virgin, a defining phrase (like, 'a man had not known her') had to be added (see Gen. 24:16; Judg. 21:12). Moreover, a *betûlah* could be widowed and mourning over a husband (Joel 1:8). The term (something like 'young gals') sometimes appears along with 'young fellows' (*baḥûr/baḥûrîm;* Deut. 32:25; 2 Chron. 36:17; Ps. 148:12; Jer. 31:13; 51:22; Ezek. 9:6; Amos 8:13; Zech. 9:17) and other groups as an 'age' category. Gordon Wenham insists that the age consideration seems primary and argues that 'girl of marriageable age' rather than 'virgin' is the right meaning for *betûlah*.[6]

If Isaiah wanted to specify an unmarried girl/virgin in verse 14, then *'almah* was his best choice.[7]

2. 'Rejecting evil and choosing good' in verses 15 and 16a. The expression should be carefully observed. The Immanuel-figure will possess a *consistently godly character*. This is *not* a reference to mere discrimination, as in Deuteronomy 1:39 ('your sons who do not know today good and evil'). Isaiah rather speaks of the child's *refusing* evil and *choosing* good. This is not simply moral discernment – it is *godly determination*.[8]

---

6. See his summary in ISBE 4:989; see also M. Tsevat, TDOT, 2:340-41.

7. If the sign Yahweh offered Ahaz could be of staggering proportions (v. 11), one might then suppose that the sign he imposed (14a) would be staggering as well (14b). cf. Alec Motyer, *Isaiah*, Tyndale Old Testament Commentaries (Leicester: Inter-Varsity, 1999), p. 77. An unmarried girl/ virgin giving birth would be just a bit phenomenal.

8. E. J. Young, 1:292, is one of the few commentators who seems to see that this phraseology refers to character.

Immanuel then will be everything Ahaz and his lackeys were not. Ahaz chose evil (alliance under Assyria) and not good (trust in Yahweh's word of promise).

3. Purpose or result, not time, in verse 15b. The Hebrew verb form in verse 15b is an infinitive of the verb 'to know' (the form used is *lĕdaʻtô*). Most English versions translate this verb form in a temporal, time-oriented sense. Typical renderings are: 'by the time he knows,' 'when he knows,' 'until he knows.' However, Joseph Jensen notes that whenever this infinitive is used with the prefixed preposition *lĕ* (as here), it always expresses result or purpose and never time (more than forty occurrences involved).[9] That means no 'when' or 'until' or time-element should be used in translating verse 15b. Rather the child eats curds and honey *'so that* he may know rejecting evil and choosing good.' That may still perplex. It seems to imply that the child will eat the diet of a ravaged land and that that will in some way shape and/ or re-inforce his godly character (cf. Deut. 8:3). In any case, there is *no time indicator*. William Dumbrell sums up the significance of Jensen's study:

> Consider that the latter half of 7:15 may [should!] be translated as a purpose clause ..., as Joseph Jensen ... argues, and not as a temporal clause. Then the announced birth of a child to a young woman (7:14) could involve a reversal of Israel's fortunes in the far-distant future (i.e., far beyond the immediate Assyrian crisis), and be a promise that concerns the house of David, finally (cf. 7:13), more than it does Ahaz, the current ruler.[10]

---

9. See the important article by Joseph Jensen, 'The Age of Immanuel,' *Catholic Biblical Quarterly* 41 (1979), especially pp. 227-31. I checked sixteen English versions on Isaiah 7:15 – only two (AV/KJV and NKJV) got it right.

10. William J. Dumbrell, *The Faith of Israel*, 2nd ed. (Grand Rapids: Baker, 2002), p. 111.

When verse 15 is freed of a time-element one no longer needs to grub around in a fruitless search to dig up some child contemporary with Ahaz.

4. Verse 16 is still bad news. This verse is usually taken as a somewhat parenthetical but basically positive reaffirmation of Isaiah's assurance to Ahaz in verses 4-9: the threat of Syria and Israel against you will soon evaporate.[11] Ahaz is 'in dread' of these kings but they will soon be off the scene.

But there are problems with this interpretation. It is usually assumed that the 'land' (lit., ground) that will be 'forsaken' refers to Syria and Israel (Ephraim), the 'land' of the two kings, Rezin and Pekah. But the word is not plural but singular ('land'), a weird way to refer to the very distinct territories of Syria and Israel. One would expect a plural if that were the meaning. And then 'to be in dread' may not be the better rendering of the verb form (*qwṣ*). There may be two verbs with that root.[12] The root occurs in verse 6; it could mean, 'to cause dread, terrify,' or 'to tear up, apart.' I have translated it as the latter – note that the parallel verb in verse 6 is a synonymous 'to break open' (*bāqaʿ*). That is the big talk of Rezin and Pekah: 'Let us tear it [Jerusalem] up and break it open for ourselves.' Now the same root apparently appears in verse 16, and it seems more natural to take it, not as an attitude Ahaz has ('of which you are in dread'), but as an action he is perpetrating, i.e., 'the land (or, ground) you are *tearing apart* (by your unbelieving policies).'[13] Then the 'land' or 'ground' refers to the one land of Judah and

11. See, e.g., H. C. Leupold, *Exposition of Isaiah*, 2 vols. (Grand Rapids: Baker, 1968), 1:159-60; also Young, 1:292-93.

12. See K-B, 1089-90; NIDOTTE, 3:906.

13. On this see especially Murray R. Adamthwaite, 'Isaiah 7:16 – Key to the Immanuel Prophecy,' *The Reformed Theological Review* 59.2 (2000): pp. 65-73. See also the article by J. Barton Payne cited in note 1, and the commentaries of John MacKay, Gary Smith, and Allan Harman.

Ephraim (i.e., to Israel as a whole) and being forsaken of 'both its kings' means that not only will the northern kingdom bite the dust but Judah and the dynasty of David will go belly up as well. Hence far from being a parenthetical positive reassurance verse 16 is a judgment-word and fits consistently then in the flow of verses 15-17. Though one could not see it at the time (734 B.C.), verse 16 (land forsaken of both its kings) takes us down the time-line, past the fall of Samaria and then of Judah into the exile to Babylon. That will happen *before* this Immanuel-figure is extant and rejecting evil and choosing good. Again, Immanuel is someone *beyond* Ahaz and *removed from* Ahaz.[14]

In summary, then, verses 15-17 seem to say that Immanuel will exist when the nation is in reduced and desolate conditions (v. 15), a time after kingship in both Israel and Judah has become defunct (v. 16), and certainly therefore after the more

---

14. I am not denying that, in general, the Immanuel prophecy is good news; I am only saying that *in this context* it is bad news for Ahaz in that, clearly, this 'Immanuel' is someone not available to Ahaz. Biblical prophecy may do this – use a positive message in a negative way. For example, note Micah 3:12: 'Therefore, because of you Zion will be turned into a ploughed field, Jerusalem a heap of ruins, and the temple mount an overgrown height.' This is the judgment announced to the corrupt and blood-shedding leadership in the southern kingdom (roughly contemporary with Isaiah). Then immediately after this, in 4:1-4, Micah places a word of hope, which begins: 'And it shall be at the end of the days [that] the mountain of Yahweh's house will be established as the highest of the mountains, and it shall be lifted up above [the] hills and peoples shall flow up to it' (Micah 4:1). The very place Micah had said would be devastated and denuded he then promises will become the magnetic center of Yahweh's kingdom. But note that he says this latter will be 'at the end of the days', that is, down the time-line in the future and *removed from* the current ungodly generation. They will have no part in this hope. In that sense, the marvelous coming restoration of 4:1-4 is a judgment word to the current generation, for they will have no part in it. The devastation of 3:12 awaits them and the hope of 4:1-4 has been put beyond their reach, and so both words function as bad news for them.

immediate scourge, the king of Assyria (v. 17). If this is correct, then we needn't mess with 'double fulfillment' schemes nor scurry around trying to dredge up some contemporary (8th century B.C.) *'almah* – or Immanuel – candidate to fill the need of a non-existent relevance for Ahaz.

Issue of the prophecy

The major matter in this prophecy is the question of *faith*. In whom would Ahaz, the royal house, and the people of Judah trust? In Yahweh's promise (vv. 7-9) or in Assyria's power? Who is the Savior in our distress? Ahaz clearly preferred Tiglath-pileser, as his appeal to him in 2 Kings 16:7 shows: 'Come up and save me from the hand of the king of Syria and from the hand of the king of Israel.' This brought short-term relief (2 Kings 16:8-9) but unparalleled (see Isa. 7:17) and ongoing desolation (Isa. 7:18-25).

One can imagine how Ahaz's pro-Assyrian counselors advised him: 'Look, Isaiah deals in words, in theology, in abstractions; he's all right in his place. But this is politics; we are having to play international hardball. We can't afford to dabble in mere talk. Diplomacy is our only hope. We must simply pay Tiglath-pileser a huge bribe and ask him to knock off Syria and Israel.' Faith was not for Ahaz. Bribing the king of Assyria was a sure thing, and he was going to go for it.

We seem prone to place our confidence in rulers of one ilk or another. At this distance we may marvel at the wild enthusiasm with which the Scots embraced that snake, Charles II, at the Restoration (ca. 1660), perhaps partly because they simply couldn't shake off their loyalty and love affair with the Stuart kings. But Charles, despite solemn promises, proves a scourge rather than a savior. On the other hand, we can understand why beleaguered believers may have been heartened when the Bolsheviks seized power, especially when they heard such statements as:

Each person must have complete freedom not only to observe any faith but also to propagate any faith …. None of the officials should even have a right to ask anyone of his faith; this is a matter of conscience and nobody should dare to interfere in this field.[15]

Ironically, that's a statement by Vladimir Lenin. The rulers of this age can easily seduce our faith; they seem so much more promising than Yahweh's mere word.

The impact of this prophecy: the secret of steadfastness (8:9-10)

Chapter 7 depicted the unbelief of the royal house; chapter 8 shows how the believing remnant is to function in face of the coming Assyrian scourge.

But we're getting ahead of ourselves. Yahweh told Isaiah to get a large tablet and write on it 'Belonging to Maher-shalal-hash-baz.' As I've translated it, this means 'Belonging to Rush-to-plunder-speed-to-spoil,' or, adapting James Moffatt's approach, 'Spoilsoonplunderpronto.' Yahweh had witnesses pegged (v. 2) to attest what the prophet had written and when he had done so. These witnesses may not have been pro-Isaiah; for example, Uriah was likely the wishy-washy high priest serving under Ahaz (see 2 Kings 16:10-16). It might be crucial to have someone who could attest that Isaiah had written this 'message' *before* it began to be fulfilled. It was not something Isaiah concocted after the fact.

Now what sort of message was this? Imagine a teenage lad coming home at lunch-time and telling his family, 'I just saw Isaiah holding up a billboard down at the intersection. It said, "Maher-shalal-hash-baz." What do you suppose that's all about?' As Motyer says, Isaiah's placard was 'intended to provoke questions, not to answer them.'[16]

---

15. Cited in James and Marti Hefley, *By Their Blood: Christian Martyrs of the Twentieth Century*, 2nd ed. (Grand Rapids: Baker, 1996), p. 227.

16. J. Alec Motyer, *The Prophecy of Isaiah* (Downers Grove, IL: Inter-Varsity, 1993), p. 90.

Then the prophet and Mrs Isaiah have a son. Immanuel had no relevance to King Ahaz but this child does – and to Judah as well. But one cringes for the poor wee fellow: Yahweh tells Isaiah to give him the billboard name: Maher-shalal-hash-baz. Yet the drastic name is good news to folks in Judah, for it means that before the lad acquires the basic language skills of 'Daddy' and 'Mommy', the king of Assyria will have carted off the 'spoil' and 'plunder' of Damascus and Samaria (v. 4). The Syro-Ephraimite alliance would no longer be an item. Relief indeed. And so it was. In 733 Tiglath-pileser overran Israelite turf in Galilee and east of the Jordan, deporting populations and destroying cities; then, in 732, he ravaged Damascus, executing Rezin.[17]

However, a kid with a name like Spoilsoonplunderpronto must signal bad news for someone. And so he did. That's the point of verses 5-8. There is debate over verse 6. I take it as speaking of the people of Judah and their apparently ecstatic joy over Assyria's overthrow of Rezin and Pekah. They may have been exchanging high-fives over what they regarded as Ahaz's suave and successful foreign policy maneuvers.[18] So they, in essence, were aping the king's unbelieving trust in Assyrian muscle. Isaiah compares Yahweh's promise (7:7-9) to 'the waters of Shiloah', the little stream that flows from the Gihon spring on the west side of the Kidron Valley. That option was despised; instead, Ahaz and Judah wanted the might of the Euphrates ('the River,' 8:7) – and they would get it. They would get more of Assyria than they bargained for. Like a flood Assyria would inundate Judah, simply keep on coming, until Judah could hardly keep her chin above water level (vv. 7-8); indeed, Judah will suffer a kind of national asphyxiation. At the end of this threat, Isaiah drops a name. He says that the

---

17. John Bright, *A History of Israel*, 3rd ed. (Philadelphia: Westminster, 1981), pp. 274-75.

18. Here I follow John Oswalt and Gary Smith.

'outstretching of [Assyria's] wings shall fill the breadth of your land, O Immanuel' (v. 8b). He picks up the name of Yahweh's sign, of the royal child of 7:14. He is not yet on the historical scene. But Isaiah recalls the promise. He assumes 'the land' belongs to him. He speaks as if, somehow, the future Immanuel matters in the present moment.

How? Well, if Assyria is going to overrun not only Syria and Israel but also choke Judah within an inch of its life, one has to ask how Yahweh's true people will fare in such times. What does God's remnant do when he judges their whole nation? Verses 9-10 disclose the answer. We can understand Isaiah, as a representative of the believing remnant, speaking the words of verses 9-10. As such they 'address' Assyria or, indeed, any peoples:[19]

(9) Do your worst, O peoples,
      and be shattered;
      and listen, all distant places of the earth:
          Get yourselves ready and be shattered!
          Get yourselves ready and be shattered!

(10) Hatch a plan – and it will be frustrated;
      speak a word – and it will never stand,
      for … Immanuel!

Here are the true disciples of Yahweh bursting forth with defiant faith in the face of Assyria's big red machine. Note the *basis* for this steadfastness in the last line: 'for Immanuel,' i.e., 'for God is with us.' Note too how their 'it will never stand' (*lō' yāqûm*, v. 10) picks up and affirms Yahweh's previous assurance to Ahaz in 7:7, 'It will not hold up/stand' (*lō' tāqûm*). The remnant believes what the king rejected. But the last line of verse 10 tells us that before Immanuel himself arrives, the remnant already

---

19. They are *not* the words of the Assyrians, as the New Living Translation interprets with its insertion (and a bad one at that) into the text.

trusts the truth he will embody. For them, Immanuel is not only a King to come but a truth to live by in the present moment. It is the secret of their steadfastness.

Someone may object: Wait a minute – you don't mean to say that a mere promise, a mere assurance that their God was with them would hold them up, do you? In the mean, harsh world of politics and 'reality'? A little over thirty years later it did. Check out 2 Kings 18–19 or Isaiah 36–37. Sennacherib, the king of Assyria, invaded, knocked off – according to Assyrian reports – forty-six of Judah's walled towns, and was ready to reduce Jerusalem. And then one night thereabouts the Angel of Yahweh wiped out 185,000 Assyrians in their sleeping bags. And Sennacherib went back home without ever entering Jerusalem. Now Sennacherib doesn't tell us in his annals that his army was wiped out like that – but then do you list your failures when you circulate your resume? Especially if you're cocky like Sennacherib? The historical fact remains – Sennacherib did not conquer Jerusalem. Why not? Well, a funny thing happened one night in the Assyrian camp. An 'Immanuel' moment.

Sometimes one runs into faint analogies of this. In October 1864, during the War between the States, Federal troops under the command of General Phil Sheridan took up position on a chain of low hills behind Cedar Creek, about twenty miles south of Winchester, Virginia. Sheridan went off for a conference in Washington. But some of Jubal Early's Confederates wormed their way through what was thought an almost impossible approach and smashed into the Federal left flank. The surprise generated a retreat that turned into a rout. Ere long the Confederates had bagged 1,300 prisoners and eighteen cannon and had driven the Federal line at least four miles back. Federal wagon trains were snarled, trying to flee from the front. Troops, alone or in groups, were ambling along to the safety of Winchester. No officer's commands seemed to command their compliance for long. But Sheridan had gotten back the night before and came riding out about nine in the morning. He was meeting tangled wagon trains, fugitives, camp followers, and stragglers – a motley, sorry excuse for an army. But everywhere Sheridan rode among them his cry was the same: 'Turn back!' Bruce Catton says the effect was electric. Everywhere men hitched up their pants, grabbed their muskets, cheered, and started back to the battlefield. For Sheridan it was a twenty mile ride on his huge black horse – waving his hat, yelling at his men, and all along the way men crying 'Sheridan! Sheridan!' at the top of their lungs. He met one panicky fellow riding for the rear as fast as his mule could carry him. Sheridan asked him how things were at the front and received the answer: 'Oh, everything is lost and gone, but it will be all right when you get there.' And that was the sentiment. All along jubilant men spun on their heels to return to the fight 'because they believed that if he was going to be there everything would be all right again.' A Vermont Brigade historian wrote: 'Such a scene as his presence produced …. No more doubt or chance for doubt existed; we were safe, perfectly and unconditionally safe, and every man knew it.'[20]

That was the emotional feeling anyway, the sense of utter security, that their general's presence gave them. In principle, that is the stance of remnant believers in Isaiah 8:9-10. This defiant faith as they face the Assyrian terror is simply explained by 'for Immanuel', i.e., for even now God is with us. And those short words, indeed that name, is the solution to all the fear of God's people in every age, to every scourge and every darkness that dogs us. It has always been so (Ps. 23:4; 139:8b). Here is what steels the soul of God's people, what fortifies them in the face of every peril: he himself has promised to be 'there' in all their trouble. In a word, Immanuel.

---

20. Bruce Catton, *A Stillness at Appomattox* (Garden City, NY: Double-day, 1953), pp. 312-15.

The fulfillment of this prophecy: the birth of Immanuel (Matt. 1:18-25)

I direct your attention to two matters in this fulfillment passage.

The biology of salvation

We find the citation of Isaiah 7:14 in verse 23. Sometimes the idea of the virginal conception and virgin birth of Jesus is downplayed. However, Matthew is *very interested* in the 'how' of Jesus' birth (note v. 18 – 'was like this …'). Already in verse 16 he had hinted at its uniqueness ('Mary, of whom [Greek: feminine singular] Jesus was born'), and he underscores it in verses 18, 20, and 25, so that the *virgin* part of the virgin prophecy sticks out like black raspberry ice cream spilled on a pistachio-colored carpet. Something is wrong if we don't see it.

It reminds me of when I was teaching in the Bible Department of a Christian college. Students would frequently come knocking on one's office door if they had a question or inquiry. Ordinarily one could manage such interruptions, unless one was under pressure to complete preparations for class or for a writing project. Once I felt terribly 'under the gun' and so plastered my office door with two or three large-print signs, like: 'Please do not disturb, working to meet deadline.' One wanted to communicate something like: 'Read this: stay out! Remember: illiteracy is a sin.' And almost as I dreaded, there came a knock on my door. With a natural irritability I told whoever it was to come in. He did. As he opened the door, this student began surveying the door and began remarking, 'My, you sure do have a lot of signs on your door!' Worth a density award.

But surely we cannot miss Matthew's emphasis here. Matthew was particularly 'taken' with the biology of our salvation. One might wonder why. Possibly to help early Christians counter the frequent slurs that hostile Jews threw against the reputation of the Christians' Savior. In their back-and-forth with Jesus in John 8, the Jews claim 'We [emphatic] have not been born of fornication' (v. 41). It is at least arguable that they are intimating that nevertheless they *have* heard there were compromising circumstances surrounding Jesus' birth. They do not come out and call him a bastard, but subtle insinuation is sometimes more telling than blatant accusation. So Matthew may be intent to give early Christians the 'info' that will help them not to be so disturbed by such attacks.

Or one might imagine Matthew himself answering such allegations: 'You want to know the circumstances of Jesus' birth? All those 'shady' details? Well, Jesus was born of the virgin Mary; not an unfaithful Mary who shacked up with somebody else, nor, in a moment of weakness, with Joseph himself. No, she was a virgin. And all this should not surprise you, because Bible prophecy had stated that the *'almah*/virgin would become pregnant and give birth to the King Immanuel. This miraculous birth had been foretold long ago, so why should this strange biology of Immanuel surprise you?'

The model of faith

I want to focus your attention on Joseph in this same passage, perhaps with some repetition from the previous section.

Major dilemma. Mary is pregnant (v. 18b), and Joseph does not yet know that the Holy Spirit has anything to do with it. It looks, sadly, like something very unholy and not done by any spirit. If he goes ahead and consummates the marriage, it will look like he himself must be the 'guilty' one. Imagine his turmoil when he first heard the news. He must have concluded there was, however briefly, someone else. Mary had been unfaithful.[21] Yet his righteousness (v. 19a) is not hard but kind;

---

21. Some may wonder how Joseph could think that of Mary. But given that in their Galilean context couples were likely allowed very little 'face time' before marriage, it may well be that Joseph and Mary did not know each other very well. See Craig S. Keener, *A Commentary on the Gospel of Matthew* (Grand Rapids: Eerdmans, 1999), p. 92. His whole section, pp. 87-95, is well worth consulting.

he had no desire to disgrace Mary, and he reached his decision (v. 19b) to divorce her quietly.

Then the word of God via the angel of the Lord shatters his careful reasoning. Note that the angel's words begin in verse 20b and run through the word 'Immanuel' in verse 23a.[22] Hence Matthew is not citing Isaiah 7:14 as a proof text for his readers (though in one sense that could be said), but the angel is citing the prophecy in his address to Joseph. He is pressing the significance of the Immanuel-word upon Joseph.

Now what may happen if Joseph follows the angel's directions? He will still have problems – perhaps worse ones. *He* may now know that Mary's pregnancy is the mysterious work of the Holy Spirit, but the people of Nazareth don't. He knew what people would say: 'Joseph must be the one or he wouldn't go ahead with the marriage; if it's not his child, then he's stupid to marry her; I surely wouldn't want some girl who had been unfaithful.' Maybe the scandal would affect his carpentry business? Did he take Mary to Bethlehem with him (Luke 2) to get her away from local ridicule? There was, in any case, a price to pay: he could divorce Mary, be completely exonerated, with his reputation intact; or, following the angel's word, he could be smeared with suspicion and innuendo the rest of his life.

Now, note verse 20 and the angel's opening words: 'Joseph, son of David, don't be afraid to take Mary ....' Note how the 'Don't be afraid' sounds strangely like Isaiah 7:4, Isaiah's call to Ahaz to cast off fear. Note especially that the angel addresses Joseph as 'son of David'. What was Ahaz but a 'son of David'? Is there not a deliberate *contrast* here? In Isaiah 7: Here is a

---

22. Here I follow D. A. Carson ('Matthew,' in *The Expositor's Bible Commentary*, 12 vols. [Grand Rapids: Zondervan, 1984], 8:76) against NIV and most versions. If the angel's words run through verse 23a, then the verb form *gegonen* in verse 22 can have its normal 'perfect tense' translation, the angel saying, 'All this *has taken place* to fulfil ....'

reigning king, Ahaz, called to trust God's word and given a blank check offer of any razzle-dazzle sign to encourage him to believe; and he won't. In Matthew 1: Here is a carpenter called to lose, perhaps, what he does have because God is fulfilling Scripture; and in faith he is willing to pay the price. At last, a son of David who believes. In Joseph we have a model of faith, who was everything Ahaz was not. And in Jesus we have Immanuel – God with us.

FAITHFUL LIVING IN A FALLING WORLD
(Isaiah 8:11-22)

(11) For here's what Yahweh said to me,
          overpowering me with his hand
              and warning me against walking in the way of this
              people, saying,

(12) 'You must not say "Conspiracy!"
          of whatever this people dubs "conspiracy,"
          and you must not fear what they fear
          nor be in dread (of it).

(13) Yahweh of hosts – he's the One you must regard as holy
          – he must be your fear,
          he must be your dread,

(14) and he shall be a sanctuary;
          as well as a stone to trip over

47

and a rock to stumble over
 for both of the houses of Israel;
 for a trap and a lure to the resident of Jerusalem.

(15) And many among them shall stumble,
 shall fall and be smashed,
 and shall be caught and captured.'

(16) Tie up the testimony,
seal up the teaching among my disciples;

(17) and I shall wait for Yahweh,
who is hiding his face from the house of Jacob,
and I shall hope for him.

(18) Look! Here I am and the children Yahweh has given me
– signs and wonders in Israel
from Yahweh of hosts
who dwells on Mount Zion.

(19) And when they say to you,
'Seek out the necromancers and those "in the know"
 that bleep and mutter
– should not a people seek its gods,
the dead on behalf of the living?'

(20) To the teaching! And to the testimony!
If they will not speak in line with this word,
then dawn will never come for them.

(21) And one shall pass through it hard-pressed and hungry,
and when he is hungry he shall go into a rage,
and he shall curse by his king and his gods;
and he shall turn his gaze upward,

(22) and he will look to the earth,
and, indeed!, distress and darkness,
 agonizing darkness,
 driven into deep darkness (Isa. 8:11-22).

Leon Morris tells of an elderly lady having her first flight in an airplane. Darkness came and so did her concern. She hailed the steward and asked, 'How does the pilot know where he is going when he is away up in the air like this and he cannot see the way?' The steward then pointed to a place outside the window where a green light was flickering on the wing. 'Do you see that green light?,' he asked. Yes, she did. He then directed her attention through a window on the opposite side. Did she see that red light over there? She certainly did. 'Well,' assured the steward, 'as long as he keeps between those two lights he is okay.'[1] A perfectly phony explanation but perhaps dispensing peace is a crafty business. But the woman's concern is both proper and perennial for God's people: How do you know how to get through the scary stuff? And there was plenty of scary stuff in the latter years of eighth-century B.C. Judah. The country was being squeezed on all sides and ere long mighty Assyria would all but wash them away (7:17; 8:7-8). How can Yahweh's remnant manage in such upheaval? What do you do if in the foreseeable future your nation is going to be crushed? What do you do if you live in a nation going to ruin because of the policy of her leaders? What then do you have, what can you cling to, what must you hold on to when you live as God's remnant in a falling nation? What ought to be true of Yahweh's remnant in such times? This text presses two considerations on us.

First, there is **the difference that defines us** (vv. 11-15). Yahweh brought immense pressure on Isaiah ('overpowering me with his hand,' v. 11b) 'warning me against walking in the way of this people' (v. 11c). Isaiah and those with him were to adopt a counter-cultural stance; they were to take up an against-the-stream position. In this segment, Yahweh is calling

---

1. Leon Morris, *Expository Reflections on the Gospel of John* (Grand Rapids: Baker, 1990), pp. 652-53.

STUMP KINGDOM – AN EXPOSITION OF ISAIAH

his remnant to walk in faith, as he had called Ahaz to walk in faith in 7:4.

The verbs in verses 12-13 are plural forms, so we know Yahweh is not speaking to Isaiah alone but to those believers associated with him. And he is calling them to a *lonely faith*:

> You must not say 'Conspiracy!'
> of whatever this people dubs 'conspiracy,'
> and you must not fear what they fear
> nor be in dread (of it) (v. 12).

Their attitude was to be directly opposite the general mood of the nation. But what is this 'conspiracy' that so preoccupies most of the folks in Judah? There are several possibilities but no one seems to know for sure. It may well refer to the coalition between Syria and Israel, designed to assault Jerusalem, dethrone Ahaz, and install Rezin and Pekah's chosen stoolie on the throne (7:1-2, 5-6). If so, Yahweh does not mean Isaiah & Co. should refuse to recognize this threat but that they should not give in to the panic and paranoia consuming the people – people who were aping the dread their leaders felt (7:2).[2] 'You must not fear what they fear.' Lonely faith can be hard. It's hard not to get caught up in the contemporary hysteria of choice.

They must also possess a *trembling faith*:

> Yahweh of hosts – he's the One you must
>   regard as holy
> – he must be your fear,
> he must be your dread (v. 13).

'Yahweh of hosts' is in emphatic position, as if to say 'Yahweh himself must be your preoccupation.' 'Of hosts' is a kind of omnipotence formula, as if to say, Yahweh has all the armies

---

2. See J. Ridderbos, *Isaiah*, Bible Student's Commentary (Grand Rapids: Zondervan, 1985), p. 96.

of heaven, all the resources available, at his disposal.[3] 'He's the One you are to regard as holy,' that is, to realize He's the God of Isaiah 6. Or, as Ortlund puts it, 'To regard as holy' means 'Dare to treat God as *God*. Don't respond to life in a way that makes God look helpless and weak and worthless.'[4] And part of what 'regarding as holy' means is that Yahweh himself becomes 'your fear' and 'your dread'. As soon as a text says something like this, someone speaks up to qualify it with 'Now that doesn't mean fear in the sense of terror.' Why not? How do they know that? What are we to assume it means when we are told Yahweh is to be our 'dread'? Why are we so concerned to make Yahweh nothing but a mild-mannered church-keeper? Why shouldn't we tremble before this God? Among other things, such trembling excludes other trembling:

> Fear him, ye saints, and you will then
> have nothing else to fear:
> make you his service your delight;
> he'll make your wants his care.[5]

Peter applies this Isaiah text to his own flock in 1 Peter 3:14-15a. Instead of fearing they are to 'reverence the Lord as holy, that is, Christ' (v. 15a; note that Peter identifies Christ with Yahweh). 'Reverencing' Christ this way 'means really to believe that Christ, not one's human opponents, is truly in control of events.'[6] Yahweh demands the same response from Isaiah and his fellow believers.

3. See J. Alec Motyer, *The Prophecy of Isaiah* (Downers Grove, IL: Inter-Varsity, 1993), pp. 44-45.

4. Raymond C. Ortlund, Jr., *Isaiah: God Saves Sinners* (Wheaton, IL: Crossway, 2005), p. 96.

5. From 'Through All the Changing Scenes of Life,' *Trinity Hymnal* (Atlanta: Great Commission, 1990), No. 624.

6. Wayne Gruden, *1 Peter*, Tyndale New Testament Commentaries (Leicester: Inter-Varsity, 1988), p. 153.

Then we might also say Yahweh calls his remnant to a *secure faith*. The first line of verse 14 tells how Yahweh will show himself to faith: 'He shall be a sanctuary.' It may be stretching the term to assume it connotes a place of asylum here. The word is *miqdāsh*. It occurs in the 'big' tabernacle text, in Exodus 25:8: 'And they shall make for me a *sanctuary*, and I shall dwell in their midst.' The sanctuary is where Yahweh dwells, and if he is there, then they are – among other matters – perfectly safe.

The believing remnant then is to take a different stance; but they will also have a different destiny (vv. 14-15). As noted, they will enjoy Yahweh as their security but unbelievers in Judah will find him a stone or rock that trips them up or a trap and lure that sucks them into helpless captivity. A bit startling: Yahweh is not the easy-going, nonchalant, domesticated deity we may imagine. The same God may be security or ruin. And this latter is not a mere possibility for people in Judah; rather, 'many among them shall stumble, shall fall and be smashed, and shall be caught and captured' (v. 15). Isaiah and his ilk are called to a faith that marks them as different in their present age. That in itself is difficult – it is much easier to blend and to 'fear what they fear.'

Ronald Reagan tells of his days when he was governor of California. It was 1969. These were the days of mayhem and demonstrations at the universities. He had to go to a meeting at the University of California campus in San Diego. He refused to use the back entrance. He got out in front and had a long walk of about 150 yards to the door of the administration building. There was a bit of a rise on either side of the walk – and both sides were packed with demonstrators, who had decided to carry out a silent protest and simply glare at Reagan as he made his lonely way to the building. As he was nearing the end of his trek a girl came down off the knoll and out of the crowd to meet him. Reagan wondered what on earth she – or they – had planned. When he approached, she was waiting for him and held out her hand. Reagan took it, and then he – and everyone – heard her break the silence with: 'I just want to tell you, I like everything you're doing as governor.'[7] The sheer guts of defying the crowd and refusing to bend to the cultural flow!

That is the kind of stance required of Yahweh's remnant. What you fear is different; your agenda is different; your preoccupations are different. It's not that you don't have any fears. You may. But your fears are, well, *different*. You fear your children might turn away from the Lord. You fear that your heart will grow cold and formal toward Christ in your advancing years. You fear that in some sudden temptation you may prove faithless. But you do not fear what 'they' fear.

We may not share Judah's precise situation – facing a hostile military coalition. If we believe politicians and pundits and polls, it sounds like folks fear economic collapse or recession or too-high taxes or not getting to keep the money they earn, or – as sometimes put in my country – not able to achieve 'the American dream' (i.e., a certain level of economic success). You must not fear what they fear. 'Yahweh of hosts … he must be your fear, he must be your dread.' There is a strange liberation in that.

Then Isaiah suggests there is a second distinguishing mark of Yahweh's remnant: **the light that directs us** (vv. 16-22).

Verse 16 is a bit of a conundrum. Some take it as God's direction to Isaiah, and some take it as Isaiah's prayer to God (the verbs are imperative singulars). It is a hard call. Verses 17-18 are clearly Isaiah's words. Verse 17 begins with, 'And I shall wait,' which may suggest continuing on from something already spoken. On balance I prefer to take verse 16 as Isaiah's words, as his prayer to Yahweh. On this view verses 16-18 are Isaiah's

---

7. Ronald Reagan, *An American Life* (New York: Simon and Schuster, 1990), pp. 181-82.

words (his prayer, v. 16, and his confession of faith, vv. 17-18)[8] and verses 19-22 could be Yahweh's warning given to Isaiah and his followers or simply Isaiah's warning given to his followers.

One can gather the main thrust of the whole segment by setting verse 16 and verses 19-20 over against one another. On the one hand, Isaiah prays Yahweh would 'tie up the testimony' and 'seal up the teaching' among his disciples. The imagery comes from the way an important scroll might be handled – tied up with a seal affixed to preserve and to prevent tampering. But Isaiah seems to use the idea figuratively: that God would so impress and apply and anchor his disciples in the word he has just given Isaiah that they will be held by it and directed by it. And this means repudiating other alleged 'guides', like necromancers and all who claim they can get light 'from beyond' (vv. 19-20). This latter option had long been off limits for Israel (Deut. 18:9-14), but there were always some plying their wares, who urged one to get in touch with the dead to find light for living, to get an edge for the way ahead. Hence Yahweh's warning:

> And when they say to you,
> 'Seek out the necromancers and those "in the know"
> that bleep and mutter … .'
> To the teaching! And to the testimony!
> If they will not speak in line with this word,
> then dawn will never come for them (vv. 19a, 20).[9]

---

8. In expressing his faith Isaiah, in verse 18, may be alluding to the names of his children. Maher-shalal-hash-baz ('Spoilsoonplunderpronto') was a walking sign of Assyria's ravaging of Syria and Israel—and of Assyria's 'suffocation' of Judah (8:3-8); Shear-jashub ('a remnant will return') pointed to a hope beyond Assyria's deprivations (cf. 10:20-23). And surely Isaiah's own name ('Yahweh saves') bears a testimony of faith.

9. I have omitted the last two lines of verse 19 here. They are difficult. In my translation (see first of chapter) I have taken them as part of the words of those urging recourse to necromancy. cf. John L. MacKay, *A Study Commentary on Isaiah*, 2 vols. (Darlington: Evangelical Press, 2008), 1:232.

54

The only safety is in the teaching and the testimony (v. 20a) already given to Yahweh's servant, Isaiah (v. 16). The word of God will hold you on a right course but pagan detours will lead to nothing but bleak, nasty, agonizing, and miserable darkness (cf. vv. 21-22).

And yet such 'alternate arts' seem to hold a perennial allure and generate undying enthusiasm to this day, whether the occultism of choice be necromancy, black magic, astrology, or whatever. Here is a Nigerian Christian pastor, Benjamin Ojobu, who 'purchased the severed head of a recently deceased young woman from a cemetery to be used as a charm for fighting witchcraft and as a special offering for prosperity.' His defense? 'Yes, I am a man of God. But I do this outside Church hours.'[10]

In his young and pre-conversion days in Zimbabwe Stephen Lungu briefly had work at a Presbyterian church. One day the pastor asked Stephen's help. The pastor had placed a large bet on a particular horse at the local race track and so wanted it to win. He needed a black-magic potion from a medicine man and asked Stephen to go collect it. So off to Borrowdale race-course. There a church elder, who worked at the race-course and doubled as a medicine man in his spare time, gave Stephen a package of horse urine, horse dung, and a horse's footprint in some mud. He was to keep it all safe and was not to look back once he left or he would dilute the charm.[11]

And one thinks of Joseph Goebbels, Hitler's propaganda guru, who called Hitler in the latter's Führerbunker to congratulate him on the death of Franklin Roosevelt. It apparently

---

10. John D. Woodbridge and Frank A. James III, *Church History, Vol. 2* (Grand Rapids: Zondervan, 2013), p. 705, citing a 2008 article in *Christianity Today*.

11. Stephen Lungu, with Anne Coomes, *Out of the Black Shadows* (Oxford: Monarch Books, 2001), pp. 59-60.

was an auspicious sign. 'It is written in the stars,' Goebbels exulted. He was depending on horoscopes that predicted the last half of April 1945 would bring an overwhelming victory for the Germans.[12] It brought a victory, but not Germany's.

But there are more sanitized and 'Christian' alternatives to the word. A pastor has counseled a professing believer, noting what the word of God requires in his/her particular dilemma, and it is not what that person wants to hear. Then comes the retort: 'Well, I've prayed and prayed and prayed about this and I just feel that ....' As if volume praying trumps scriptural testimony. Subjectivism rules the word of God. Not as blatant as necromancy perhaps but a member of the same family.

Yet the watch-word of the remnant is always 'To the teaching! And to the testimony!' (v. 20a). Only the light of the written word will carry us through the darkness of our times. This holds true whether the 'times' are dark historical times, dark personal times, or even the end of our present time. The last makes me think of the last day of Robert Bruce's life (d. 1631) and that moving scene at the breakfast table. Bruce had come down to breakfast that morning. His younger daughter, Martha, was seated beside him. He had enjoyed his meal, was musing in silence when suddenly he burst out with, 'Hold, daughter, hold; my Master calleth me.' He asked that the Bible – the large house Bible – be brought, but his sight failed and he could not read. 'Cast me up the eighth of Romans,' he cried, and he began repeating much of it from memory, till he came to the last two verses: 'I am persuaded, that neither death, nor life, nor angels, nor principalities, nor powers, nor things present, nor things to come, nor height, nor depth, nor any other creature, shall be able to separate us from the love of God, which is in Christ Jesus our Lord.' Then

---

12. Cornelius Ryan, *The Last Battle* (New York: Simon and Schuster, 1966), p. 318.

the blind, dying man ordered and declared: 'Set my finger on these words. God be with you, my children. I have breakfasted with you, and shall sup with my Lord Jesus this night. I die believing in these words.'[13] 'These words' – that is always the Christian's slogan. Only in the teaching and the testimony is there light and help and anchorage. The Christian is the man or woman who wades through the affairs of life always saying: 'Set my finger on these words.'

---

13. D. C. MacNicol, *Robert Bruce: Minister in the Kirk of Edinburgh* (orig. pub. 1907; repr. ed., Banner of Truth, 1961), p. 183.

LIGHT SHINES IN THE DARKNESS
(Isaiah 9:1-7)

(1)   But it will not be darkness for her who was in agony.
       In the former time he brought the land of Zebulun
              and the land of Naphtali into contempt,
       but in the later time he has made glorious
              the way (to) the sea,
              beyond the Jordan,
              Galilee of the nations.

(2)   The people walking in darkness
              have seen a great light;
       those dwelling in the land of deep darkness
              – light has shone on them!

(3)   You have multiplied the nation,
              you have increased its gladness;

they are glad before you
 like the gladness at harvest,
 like folks revel when they divide plunder.

(4) For the yoke of his burden
  and the rod for his shoulder,
  the staff the taskmaster uses on him
 – you have shattered
  as on the day of Midian.

(5) For every boot tramping in turmoil of battle
 and (every) cloak soaked in blood
 – it shall be for burning,
  food for fire!

(6) For a **child** has been born to us,
 a **son** has been given to us,
 and the dominion rests upon his shoulder,
 and they call his name
  Wonderful Counselor, Mighty God,
  Everlasting Father, Prince of Peace.

(7) Of the increase of (his) dominion and of peace
 there will be no end,
  upon the throne of David
  and over his kingdom
   to establish it
   and to sustain it
    in justice and in righteousness
    from now on and for all time.
 The zeal of Yahweh of hosts will accomplish this.

In 1959 a New Zealander, Desmond Oatridge, and his Australian wife, Jennifer, began Bible translation work among the Binumariens of New Guinea. This tribe had been ravaged by disease and attacks in the 1930s and now, almost thirty years later, they numbered only 150. Nine years later the Oatridges had their translation of the Gospel of Mark ready. It was the first book of Scripture the Binumariens had seen in their own language. The printed gospels arrived, and they held a ceremony to celebrate the occasion. A Binumarien blindfolded with a black cloth headed a long line of literates proceeding through the village square to the place where Desmond was reading the translated gospel. Upon arriving, the man removed the blindfold, symbolizing that since the Scriptures had come his people were no longer in darkness but could see the way.[1] Light shines in the darkness.

The beginning of Isaiah 9 follows this 'Binumarien' pattern. In 8:19-22 Isaiah and his fellow believers were warned against pursuing 'alternative revelation possibilities', like consulting the dead. That would only land them in agonizing darkness (8:20b-22). The only safety, the only light, was in the teaching and testimony Yahweh had already revealed (8:20a). Now Yahweh was about to supplement that testimony with a word about the difference a child will make for even a devastated people (9:1-7). He will prove a 'great light' for a people walking in darkness. What is Isaiah concerned to tell us here?

First, he wants us to see **the grace that never lets go** (vv. 1-2). Isaiah begins with a brief promise of a turn-around: 'It will not be darkness for her who was in agony' (v. 1a); but then he plunges into geography, all about Zebulun and Naphtali and terms describing those areas. These were both northern tribes, Naphtali sitting to the west of what (in the New Testament) we call the Sea of Galilee but also extending maybe 25-30 miles north of it as well; Zebulun was smaller in scope and stood at the southwest border of Naphtali. The problem with being Naphtali and Zebulun was that their turf was first stop for any invader coming in from the north (which most did), as Tiglath-pileser III did in 733/732 B.C. (see 2 Kings 15:29).

---

1. *Searchlight on Bible Words* (Huntington Beach, CA: Wycliffe Bible Translators, 1972), p. 28.

When the boiling Assyrian pot spilled over, this area was first to be scalded. It was at that time that Yahweh 'brought into contempt' Zebulun and Naphtali.[2] And the northern kingdom became a rump kingdom, little more than a sphere of influence around Samaria, until Shalmaneser V and Sargon II finished it off around 722-720 B.C. (cf. 2 Kings 17:1-6).

This is what Yahweh has done 'in the former time,' but 'in the later time' all will be changed: 'in the later time he has made glorious the way to the sea ....' Strictly speaking, the verbs in verses 1b-2 are in the 'past' tense: 'he has made glorious,' 'have seen' a great light, light 'has shone' on them. But they are describing what takes place in the 'later time', in the future. They could then be translated as futures (as John MacKay does); yet the 'past tense' form may be deliberate – to express that what is coming is so certain that it can be described as having already occurred. And Matthew quotes these verses as being fulfilled when Jesus went to Capernaum 'in the area of Zebulun and Naphtali' (Matt. 4:13) to inaugurate his ministry and proclaim the nearness of the kingdom (see Matt. 4:12-17). The very region that had been plunged into the abyss of Assyrian darkness and devastation was to be the first to see the 'great light' of the Sun of righteousness in his teaching and testimony.

I think we need to pay attention to this geography. These very northern tribes were told that glory and light would come to them through the child to be born and the son to be given. And yet in Isaiah's own time these areas will be plun-

---

2. Some think that the last three locales of verse 1 correspond to the provinces into which the Assyrians carved up northern Israel: the 'way (to) the sea' was around Dor on the Mediterranean coast; 'beyond the Jordan' was essentially Gilead to the east; and 'Galilee of the nations' was the province of Megiddo, which took in the turf of Naphtali, Zebulun, and Issachar. See Y. Aharoni, *The Land of the Bible*, rev. ed. (Philadelphia: Westminster, 1979), pp. 374-75, or, conveniently, Derek Thomas, *God Delivers: Isaiah Simply Explained* (Darlington: Evangelical Press, 1991), p. 83.

dered and pulverized – and deported – by Tiglath-pileser III (2 Kings 15:29), and soon (722) Samaria will fall, the northern kingdom will be wiped off the map, with deportation still the Assyrian policy (cf. 2 Kings 17:1-6). It was Yahweh's judgment – the northern kingdom was one, 200-year-plus exercise in apostasy (cf. 2 Kings 17:7ff.). True, early on, some of Yahweh's faithful ones had emigrated from the north into Judah (2 Chron. 11:13-17) and, even after the demise of the northern kingdom, some appeals from a Hezekiah or a Josiah apparently found a believing response among some remnants of people that had been allowed to remain in the land (cf. 2 Chron. 30:1-12, 18; 31:1; 34:6-7). But, on the whole, the northern kingdom seemed like a grand but futile experiment in covenant failure. One can hardly read 1 Kings 12–2 Kings 17 without a creeping sense of despair and being tempted to ask, 'Why this waste?' (cf. Matt. 26:8). And yet .... Yet here is an end of darkness promised to northern tribes who had been faithless to Yahweh and smooshed by Assyria. Indeed, it is an axiom of Old Testament 'last things' that *both* Israel and Judah will be united as one people in the time of restoration (see Jer. 3:11-18; 33:7; Ezek. 37:15-28; and note that the new covenant is to be 'cut' with 'the house of Israel and the house of Judah,' Jer. 31:31). Yahweh simply *refuses to let go* of his false and faithless people.

Moffatt Burriss is a South Carolina native and World War II veteran. He was captain of a unit of paratroopers in the 82nd Airborne. In 1993 he decided to take a trip to Europe to visit the war zones of fifty years before. He arrived in Anzio, Italy, and went to the American cemetery there. Massive. Row upon row of white crosses as far as one could see. Names and dates were on the grave markers. Fortunately, there was a directory in the reception building. If you knew a man's name, you could locate the block and row of his grave. Let me quote Burriss' own words:

I knew the names of my men all right. I'd never forgotten them. I could recall exactly what they looked like, the sound of their voices, things they had said. I visited each grave in turn, put my hand on the cool stone, and read the name, birth date, and death date. Back when they were killed, the rest of us had no time to grieve, but fifty years later, as I stood beside each grave, I wondered why I had survived and they had not. Thinking about it, I was moved to tears.[3]

Note the tenacity of memory there: 'I knew the names of my men all right. I'd never forgotten them.' That's the impression verses 1-2 give us of Yahweh. He never forgets his people. Even a people beaten down, clobbered by foreign armies, living for the most part in their own self-chosen spiritual darkness, 'dwelling in the land of deep darkness.' His grace just never lets go. 'I ask then, has God rejected his people? By no means!' (Rom. 11:1a).

Secondly, the prophet describes **the praise that has to get out** (vv. 3-5). Let's trace the overall development in these verses, and then we'll come back to the praise-element.

Isaiah first depicts the great change as *celebration*:

> You have multiplied the nation,
>> you have increased its gladness;
> they are glad before you
>> like the gladness at harvest,
>> like folks revel when they divide plunder (v. 3).[4]

Yahweh makes sure multiplied gladness keeps pace with the multiplied people. Isaiah rings the changes on 'gladness', the 'glad' root (*smḥ*) occurring three times in the verse. And he

---

3. T. Moffatt Burriss, *Strike and Hold* (Washington, D.C.: Potomac Books, 2000), p. 4.

4. The traditional Hebrew text has a negative in the second line: 'You have *not* increased its gladness,' but the margin suggests we read what is a similar-sounding term meaning 'to it,' i.e., 'to it you have increased gladness.' Context implies that this latter option is almost certainly correct. For another similar possibility, cf. Gerard Van Groningen, *Messianic Revelation in the Old Testament* (Grand Rapids: Baker, 1990), p. 541n.

gives us pictures of this gladness – it's like farm-gladness and war-gladness, like the relief and happiness when the harvest is all in, and like enjoying victory in war and getting to 'divvy up' the goodies taken in plunder. But this is not some rampage of merely secular delirium. It is 'before you'. 'They are glad before you,' that is, in your presence and in acknowledgement that Yahweh is the gladness-Giver.[5]

Verse 4 begins with the causal particle 'For,' giving the reason for the celebration of verse 3, namely, *liberation*. The language ('yoke of his burden,' 'rod for his shoulder,' 'staff' of the 'taskmaster') conjures up memories of Israel's bondage in Egypt (cf. Lev. 26:13; Ps. 81:6; Exod. 3:7; 5:6, 10, 13). But Yahweh shatters all this hardware of slavery 'as on the day of Midian'. Here we are meant to pull up Judges 6–8 from our memory banks. We're meant to ponder the ongoing, life-bleeding incursions of the Midianites *et al.* (Judg. 6:1-6), the ludicrously puny posse allowed to Israel (7:1-8), and the resounding, total victory God gave Gideon (7:19–8:12). It was one of those affairs with an 'only Yahweh' explanation (cf. 7:2).

Now Isaiah adds the explanation (note the 'For' in v. 5a) for the liberation: *pacification* (v. 5). The joy (v. 3) and freedom (v. 4) are possible because of a divine arms embargo (v. 5). Yahweh doesn't merely eliminate bows and spears and tanks and bombers (Ps. 46:9) but even sends up in smoke the footwear and blood-soaked clothes of individual troops. Even combat boots and ammunition vests will be toast.[6] Celebration. Liberation. Pacification. These are the prevailing conditions that the messianic king (v. 6) will bring about.

---

5. See John N. Oswalt, *The Book of Isaiah, Chapters 1-39*, New International Commentary on the Old Testament (Grand Rapids: Eerdmans, 1986), p. 243.

6. Verses 3-4 imply that the conditions of verse 5 come about because Yahweh will impose them, not because some anemic United Nations' resolution suggests them.

Now let's return to verses 3-5 as a whole. Notice that this text is not mere description but *praise*. There are second-person singular verb forms in verses 3-4: you have multiplied the nation; you have increased its gladness; you have shattered yoke, rod, and staff. This 'you' is obviously Yahweh, and so as he relates what conditions will prevail under Messiah's reign, the prophet is at the same time exulting in Yahweh as the One bringing these conditions about and praising him for doing so. I know. It's such a simple observation. Obvious. But we so easily miss it. Scripture doesn't merely want us to understand what it says, but to pull praise out of us for what it says.

James Waddell was preaching in the 1760s and 1770s in the 'Northern Neck' of Virginia. Once he was preaching when a number of sailors were in the service. His text was from John 21 and Jesus' words to Peter, 'Simon, son of Jonah, lovest thou me?' Some of the sailors were moved to tears by the preacher's appeals. At one point in his sermon, Waddell asked – in his graphic way – 'And what does Peter say?' At that point an old sailor, whose name was Peter, stood at his seat in the congregation and with tears falling down his cheeks, gave his answer: 'Lord, thou knowest all things; thou knowest that I love thee.'[7]

It was as if he was 'pulled in' – he just 'had' to respond. And the way Isaiah mixes praise with description instructs us to do the same. Surely there is joy (v. 3), relief (v. 4), and security (v. 5), but we must be eager and careful to declare who has brought it about.

Next Isaiah comes to the climax of this prophecy as he announces **the Child who makes a difference** (vv. 6-7c). Verse 6 is the third verse in a row to begin with the Hebrew particle *kî*, often translated 'For ...,' because it frequently supplies a reason or explanation. In verse 4 it provided the reason for

---

7. Henry Alexander White, *Southern Presbyterian Leaders 1683-1911* (reprint ed.; Edinburgh: Banner of Truth, 2000), p. 61.

the celebration of verse 3, namely, liberation; in verse 5, it gave the reason or further explanation of the liberation in verse 4, namely, pacification. But the 'For' in verse 6a is climactic and, as it were, explains everything! Explains the change from darkness to light in verses 1-2; explains the joy of verse 3, the freedom of verse 4, and the peace of verse 5. There are two emphatic nouns in 6a that tell all: 'For a *child* has been born to us, a *son* has been given to us.' Ray Ortlund has nicely picked up the flow of thought here: 'God's answer to everything that has ever terrorized us is a child. The power of God is so far superior to the Assyrians and all the big shots of this world that he can defeat them by coming as a mere child.'[8] And Isaiah uses most of his ink telling us about his name (v. 6b) and his regime (v. 7a-c).

The child has a four-fold name. The first segment of it is 'Wonderful Counselor' (or, Wonder-Counselor, or Wonder of a Counselor). The 'wonder' element implies deity – it is really equivalent to 'supernatural'. That is the sense of the root in Genesis 18:14. Can ninety-year-old, post-menopausal Sarah really give birth? And Yahweh asks: 'Is anything too wonderful [i.e., hard, difficult, or, in effect, supernatural] for Yahweh?' In Psalm 139:6 David declares that Yahweh's all-circumstantial, all-surrounding knowledge of him is 'too wonderful for me', that is, it is utterly beyond him, incomprehensible, or as he says, so 'high' that he can't get hold of it. Again, 'wonderful' borders on 'supernatural.' In 28:29 Isaiah says that Yahweh of hosts is 'wonderful in counsel'. The use of the same kind of terminology here in verse 6 points to the child's deity. This king then will be one who can see and discern accurately the right path to take at any time – the polar opposite of the worldly-wise and bungling Ahaz (7:12-13; 2 Kings 16:7). Surely

8. Raymond C. Ortlund, Jr., *Isaiah: God Saves Sinners* (Wheaton, IL: Crossway, 2005), p. 99.

as such a counselor he would make his wisdom available to his people in all their quandaries and perplexities.

The child is also called 'Mighty God' or 'Warrior God'. There have been attempts to tone this down to something like 'God-like hero',[9] but it won't do.[10] The same phrase is used in 10:21, where it clearly refers to Yahweh (previous verse; cf. also Deut. 10:17; Jer. 32:18). If he is 'mighty God' his people know they have his protection in their weakness. Calvin puts it well:

> He is, therefore, called *the mighty God*, for the same reason that he was formerly called *Immanuel*. (Isa. vii.14.) For if we find in Christ nothing but the flesh and nature of man, our glorying will be foolish and vain, and our hope will rest on an uncertain and insecure foundation; but if he shows himself to be to us *God* and *the mighty God*, we may now rely on him with safety.[11]

When he is called 'Everlasting Father' (or 'Father of eternity', or 'Father for all time'), the 'father' image 'expresses the role of the king as he exercises care and concern on behalf of his people.'[12] We might paraphrase, 'always a father.' 'Father-like, he tends and spares us; well our feeble frame he knows.'[13] This part of the child's name perfectly balances the immediately preceding one, for if 'mighty God' speaks of his power and

---

9. See the discussion in B. B. Warfield, *Christology and Criticism* (reprint ed.; Grand Rapids: Baker, 2003), pp. 28-39.

10. See H. Kosmala, TDOT, 2:376.

11. *Calvin's Commentaries*, 22 vols. (reprint ed.; Grand Rapids: Baker, 1981), 7:310.

12. John L. MacKay, *A Study Commentary on Isaiah*, 2 vols. (Darlington: Evangelical Press, 2008), 1:243-44. Charles Briggs (*Messianic Prophecy* [1886; reprint ed.; Peabody, MA: Hendrickson, 1988], p. 200) argues for 'father [i.e., distributor] of booty.' He takes *'ad* (more often 'everlasting' or 'perpetuity') as another word meaning 'booty' or 'spoil'; see DCH, 6:269. Though plausible (given some 'military' context), his view seems less likely.

13. From Henry Lyte's 'Praise, My Soul, the King of Heaven.'

might to fight for and defend his people, 'always a father' speaks of the tenderness and heavenly anxiety he has to care for them in all their circumstances.

Then he is 'Prince of Peace.' We can easily mislead ourselves here. Isaiah is not speaking of 'inner peace' as we in the (psychological) west often do. He means a peace in this nasty world. Verses 4-5 supply the context: he means peace in a world of oppression, war, and combat. And to bring peace in such a world is no namby-pamby affair – such peace comes by force (see Pss. 2:9 and 46:9). One of my professors in grad school used to tell of a Jewish friend of his who had a classic definition of 'peace' (Hebrew, *shalom*). His friend told him: '*Shalom* means we win, you lose!' He was saying that peace presupposes *victory*, indeed, it may be nearly synonymous with it. Do you recall what Gideon said to the men of Penuel when they refused to give Gideon and his men supplies so they could track down the rest of the Midianites? 'When I return *in peace*, I will rip down this tower' (Judg. 8:9). Did he mean he would return 'peacefully'? Clearly not. He meant: When I return *in victory*, after crushing the rest of the Midianites. Peace comes in the wake of victory, when all opposition is taken out of the way. 'Prince of peace' then does not mean that the prince is peaceful but that he has power to bring and enforce peace, even in a world where many don't care to have it.

So that is the Child's 'name' – his character, his nature, and his way with his people. We should pause a bit here. I think of how Bethan Lloyd-Jones recalled her mother once teaching an elderly gentleman, a Mr Matthews, to read. She taught him through Welsh. But he was apparently a fast learner. In almost no time Mr Matthews was reading 'slowly and haltingly' with his finger following the words. Then soon with ease. But when he first picked out the word Jesu (Jesus), he broke down, tears coursing down his cheeks, exclaiming: 'Oh, his name, his blessed name!' He picked up the book and kissed the name.[14] Shouldn't there be a spillover for us? Can we really stand before Isaiah's delineation of the Child's name and remain unmoved? Can we hear of his guidance and power and affection and not feel we are being wrenched to adoration? 'Oh, his name, his blessed name!' It is well to hear his name; it is better to hear his name and be overcome by it.

Isaiah goes on to describe the Child's rule or regime (v. 7a-c): it will be *final* ('Of the increase of [his] dominion and of peace there will be no end … from now on and for all time'), *covenantal* ('upon the throne of David and over his kingdom'; cf. 2 Sam. 7:12-16), and *just* ('in justice and in righteousness'). John Oswalt sums it up well:

> Again, it becomes clear that Isaiah has an eschatological figure in mind. This person will not be a king among kings in Israel. Rather, he will be the final king, the king to end all kings. Thus the prophet envisions the ideal Davidic monarch.[15]

We must not be satisfied with less than Isaiah's prediction. Pundits and politicians are forever offering us poor substitutes. In early 1945 Franklin Roosevelt began an unprecedented fourth term as President of the United States; Germany and Japan were about to bite the dust in defeat. So in his inaugural remarks, FDR said, 'The great fact to remember is that the trend of civilization itself is forever upward.'[16] Sorry, it's not. Not even if a president says it. Not even if you spell 'civilization' with a capital C, as if it has a quasi-divine character to it. We should be seeing enough now to know that 'civilization' is pretty much in the tank. In

---

14. Lynette G. Clark, *Far Above Rubies: The Life of Bethan Lloyd-Jones* (Ross-shire: Christian Focus, 2015), p. 129.

15. Oswalt, p. 248.

16. Jay Winik, *1944: FDR and the Year that Changed History* (New York: Simon and Schuster, 2015), p. 508.

any case, it is a slimy, ephemeral substitute for a righteous dominion that has no end.

But let us not lose sight of what Isaiah hammers into us at the beginning of verse 6: This hope, this change, this grand reversal comes because of a *Child*. Not exactly where we would be prone to start looking for help. Cat Mays, the father of American baseball's star centerfielder, Willie Mays, sometimes puzzled his son by clinging to his country-like ways. He used to hide his surplus cash in the ice tray of his freezer. Willie wondered why, and Cat explained, 'If I get robbed, they won't think to look there.'[17] Sadly, it may be true of us. If we are looking for light out of darkness, freedom from bondage, a righteous kingdom that has no end, we may never think to look to a Child. But he is where it begins – feeding trough and swaddling clothes and all.

Finally, in the last line of our text Isaiah underscores **the passion that will make it happen** (v. 7d): 'The zeal of Yahweh of hosts will accomplish this.' There need be no mystery about why Isaiah tacks on this one-liner to his prophecy. Verse 7 itself seems to promise way too much. Or go all the way back to verse 1 and read forward again – and aren't you tempted to be at least slightly skeptical?

Go back to 732 B.C. and look around. Tiglath-pileser III has turned the northern segments of Israel into Assyrian provinces; the nation is left with a fief around Samaria; the southern kingdom has been hammered by incursions of Philistines and Edomites; and it has the misfortune to be led by Ahaz and his timid and trembling administration who are trusting themselves to the tender mercies of the Assyrians. The name of the game is 'bleak'. None of this (= vv. 1-7) looks like it has a ghost of a chance of coming about. No wonder

---

17. James S. Hirsch, *Willie Mays: The Life, The Legend* (New York: Simon and Schuster, 2010), p. 547.

the change was billed 'as on the day of Midian' (v. 4), for that time in Judges 6–7 was the time of Israel's hopelessness – yet it was a day of man's weakness that became the time of God's power. So Yahweh does not trim his promises to what looks conceivable. Why should he do that? No, he gives this promise of Messiah's rule in that eighth century fiasco, exactly when circumstances looked most unlikely; and he knows you are going to have trouble believing it, so he includes his 'jealous' clause: the 'jealousy,' or 'zeal,' of Yahweh of hosts will accomplish this. He wants us to know that what may seem unbelievable is not only credible but certain. That 'zeal' is heaven's hot and holy energy to get things done. It is Yahweh's 'burning passion' to pull off his plans.

Even on a merely human level we are constantly running into impossibilities that become possible. A few weeks ago, during the college football 'bowl' games in the USA, Oregon and Texas Christian University were playing in the Alamo Bowl. TCU was without its first-string quarterback – he had been suspended because of a fight in a bar two days before the game. So TCU plays under their second-string quarterback. Oregon rolls all over them in the first half and leads TCU 31-0 at half-time. It was hopeless. I had watched the first half, but, since it was such a blow-out, I went to bed. But TCU didn't. They came out and scored thirty-one unanswered points to tie the game at the end of regulation. Then there were *three* overtimes, and in the third one TCU came out the winner, 47-41. No one would've ever guessed.

So, bleak as it looks in 732, the celebration, liberation, and pacification will all come true, as will the dominion, the throne, and the justice. The burning passion of Yahweh of hosts will see to it. There is nothing like certainty to stir your faith.

NOW, IN THE MEANTIME ...
(Isaiah 9:8–10:4)

(8)   The Lord has sent a **word** against Jacob
      and it shall fall upon Israel,

(9)   and the people shall know—all of them
      – Ephraim and the resident of Samaria—
      in arrogance and insolence of heart
      (they are) saying,

(10) 'Bricks have fallen
      but we'll build with specially cut stones;
      sycamores have been hacked down
      but we'll change them out with cedars.'

(11) So Yahweh raised up the adversaries of Rezin
            against him,
      and he stirred up his enemies,

(12) Aram to the east and Philistia to the west,
and they consumed Israel with open mouth;
for all this his anger has not turned away
but his hand is stretched out still.

(13) But **the people** have not turned back
to the One who struck (them),
and they did not seek **Yahweh of hosts**,

(14) so Yahweh cut off from Israel head and tail,
palm branch and bulrush,
in one day.

(15) The elder and the honorable man
– he's the head;
and the prophet, the teacher of lies,
he is the tail.

(16) And so it happened
that those leading this people are leading
them astray,
and those who are led are being swallowed up.

(17) Therefore the Lord will not be glad
over their young men
and he will not have compassion
on their orphans and widows,
for all of them are godless and evildoers
and every mouth speaks wicked folly;
for all this his anger has not turned away
but his hand is stretched out still.

(18) To be sure, wickedness burns like fire,
it consumes thorn-bushes and briers;
then it ignites the thickets of the forest
and they roll up in a column of smoke.

(19) Because of the fury of Yahweh of hosts the land
is scorched;

and the people have become like fuel for the fire;
no one has pity on anyone else.

(20) They cut (meat) on the right and remain famished,
and they eat on the left and are not satisfied;
each man—they eat the flesh of their own seed.

(21) Manasseh Ephraim; and Ephraim Manasseh
– together they are against Judah.
For all this his anger has not turned away
but his hand is stretched out still (Isa. 9:8-21).

(1) Woe to those who decree wicked decrees
and the writers who write misery

(2) to turn aside the poor from (making) a plea
and to rob the afflicted of my people of a just decision,
that widows might become their spoil
and that they might make orphans their plunder.

(3) But what will you do on the day of punishment?
And at the ruin that comes from far away?
To whom will you flee for help?
And where will you abandon your wealth?

(4) Nothing to do but crouch down in the place
     where prisoners are
and they will fall where those killed fall;
for all this his anger has not turned away
but his hand is stretched out still (Isa. 10:1-4).

We were once serving not in a church-planting work but in
what I would call a 'church-watering' situation. The church
had been planted but was still relatively small. We met for
morning worship in a local elementary school and had Sunday
evening worship in a Deacon's home. One Sunday evening we
were driving home from 'church', and one of our sons (about
thirteen at the time) indicated how depressed he became on

Sunday nights. Explanation followed. All was well at Sunday evening worship and afterwards, when our boys got to pow-wow with their church friends. But now that we were heading home, well, it was a sign that it was all over and one had to stare full in the face the dread of Monday at school. And that was a downer.

The sequence from 9:1-7 to 9:8–10:4 is a bit like that. We've just received the welcome description of the 'Sunday' kingdom, the word of the light and joy and security and justice of the Child's coming regime (9:1-7) only to find ourselves dropped among a people who are hammered, depleted, frustrated, and doomed (9:8–10:4). As if to say, 'Yes, that is the kingdom that is coming, but, in the meantime, this is how it is.' And the focus seems to be on the northern kingdom, usually called 'Israel' in such contexts (note the references to 'Ephraim,' the tribal name often used for the northern kingdom, and the 'resident of Samaria', the northern capital, in verse 9; the mention of 'Israel' in verses 12 and 14; and the allusions to Ephraim and Manasseh in verse 21). One might say that 9:8–10:4 forms a kind of parallel to 8:11-22. That passage is a kind of 'downer' passage on how things were in the southern kingdom of Judah. Then, there is the darkness-to-light prophecy of the Child's kingdom (9:1-7), followed by another 'downer' text of what it's like in the northern kingdom. It's almost as if two negative passages (8:11-22 and 9:8–10:4) are the wrappers for the messianic promise of 9:1-7.

Structurally, 9:8–10:4 breaks down into four distinct segments by means of the repeated refrain: 'for all this his anger has not turned away but his hand is stretched out still' (9:12, 17, 21, and 10:4). The use of the verb 'fall' (*nāphal*) in 9:8 and 10:4 may function as an 'opener' and 'closer' verb for the whole overall unit. But it is more essential to grasp the transition of thought, namely, there are those who don't give a rip about the promised kingdom run by 'the Child', and so they are eager to have their own kingdom and to make their own way – and here (9:8–10:4) is a glimpse of what that looks like.

The passage breaks down into two broad divisions, the first focusing on **the people God depicts**.

Notice that the first segment depicts Israel in her *irrational arrogance* (9:8-12). Isaiah 'quotes' Israel's attitude in verse 10. Some might call it resilience or perseverance, but the Lord labels it arrogance and insolence (v. 9). The nation is going to pot (v. 10). One can get a taste of this by re-reading 2 Kings 15. Alec Motyer summarizes it well when he says that Israel's 'internal collapse (2 Kings 15, 17) was seen in that six kings reigned during the final twenty years, four reigns ended in assassination and only one king passed the throne to his son.'[1] The nation withers but hubris thrives. If the bricks have been knocked down, we'll use specially hewn stones; if local, inferior sycamore-fig wood has been hacked to pieces, we'll import cedars from Lebanon (v. 10). If our Fords are toted to the junk yard, we'll drive BMWs.

Such pride was not ignored. The text is a bit puzzling but seems to indicate that Yahweh in turn brought the Assyrians ('the adversaries of Rezin') against Israel (v. 11a), as well as stirring up Israel's traditional enemies, Aram and Philistia, against them (vv. 11b-12a), these latter ones squeezing and eating them up from both east and west.[2] None of this scourging, however, brought repentance but only this overweening arrogance – and

---

1. Alec Motyer, *Isaiah*, Tyndale Old Testament Commentaries (Leicester: Inter-Varsity, 1999), p. 92.

2. Rezin, of course, was king-pin of the Aramaeans in Damascus. Although he later was in an alliance with Pekah of Israel (Isa. 7:1), Rezin may have previously overrun and taken Trans-jordan from Israel (cf. NBD, 3rd ed., 67) and on that basis pressed Pekah into an alliance with him. So part of Aram's (Syria's) decimation of Israel (v. 12a) could have come from Rezin as well. Or, verse 11 may refer to earlier Syrian attacks, perhaps during Menahem's reign (752–42 B.C.); on this, see Robert B. Chisholm, Jr., *Handbook on the Prophets* (Grand Rapids: Baker, 2002), p. 41.

Isaiah's point seems to be that if you see it in its true setting it is utterly insane.

But one commonly runs into this chemistry of hopelessness and arrogance. It is mid-April 1945. Berlin. Hordes of Soviet troops are pressuring the German 9th army. Berlin's days are numbered. Hitler's suicide some two weeks in the future. Reichminister Albert Speer summons General Reymann to his offices to demand an explanation of something Reymann had ordered to be done. Reymann informed Speer that he was building a landing strip between the Brandenburg Gate and the Victory Column. They needed one that was semi-secure, out of reach (for the time being) of the Soviets. Speer, however, was furious — they were hacking down Speer's ornamental bronze lamp posts to make right-of-way for the air-strip. He would not have it. 'You do not seem to realize that I am responsible for the reconstruction of Berlin,' Speer said.[3] The Third Reich is disintegrating. In practically no time Soviet troops will overrun Berlin. And Speer actually imagines that *he* will be heading up the city's reconstruction? It's both obviously zany and implicitly arrogant. That is the situation in Israel. To say, 'Sycamores have been hacked down but we'll change them out with cedars,' sounds bold and up-beat; but Isaiah would probably say it's on the same level as saying, 'We've worked in the sewers all day, but we'll slap on some after-shave and go to the party.'

Next, 9:13-17 depicts Israel with her *perverted leadership.* The people were not repentant when Yahweh sent preliminary judgments (v. 13), so Yahweh decimated the nation's leadership, as Isaiah says, 'head and tail,' or, as we might say, from top to bottom (v. 14). In verse 15 Isaiah defines his terms – with an edge: the elder and honorable man is the 'head', the prophet, who is a 'teacher of lies', is the tail. What hope can there be

---

3. See Cornelius Ryan, *The Last Battle* (New York: Simon and Schuster, 1966), pp. 378-79.

for a people who have no voice of truth among them? In any case, their leaders lead people astray and those who are led are swallowed up; blindness at the top brings disaster at the bottom (v. 16). And there seems to be no ray of light at all, nothing positive about the whole society – even orphans and widows stand among the 'godless and evildoers' who spout 'wicked folly' (v. 17). Clearly, leaders can be a channel of catastrophe on a people (vv. 15-16).

Such has happened many times over, not least in the church. One of the saddest examples is what occurred in the Free Church of Scotland within its first fifty years (1843–93). Some of her theological teachers had imbibed the methods and results of unbelieving biblical criticism imported from Germany, which meant that the Bible was not held to be the reliable record of God's revelation but a fallible cafeteria of human error. Granted, some of the Scots were not nearly as 'radical' as their German mentors. But there is A. B. Davidson teaching Old Testament at New College, quietly, suggestively, and non-confrontationally inculcating the 'new' views from the 1860s on. Some pressed the argument that the impact of the Bible's overall redemptive message is what matters and not the accuracy of its particular historical details. As Marcus Dods put it, the foundation was being shifted from a book (the Bible) to a Person (Christ) – though, strangely, one only knows of the Person from the book. At least privately Marcus Dods knew where this would lead; in a letter he admitted, 'The churches won't know themselves fifty years hence. It is to be hoped some little rag of faith may be left when all's done.'[4] 'And so it happened that those leading this people are leading them astray, and those who are led are being swallowed up' (v. 16).

---

4. Quote from Iain H. Murray, *A Scottish Christian Heritage* (Edinburgh: Banner of Truth, 2006), p. 386. See pp. 367-96 for Murray's whole treatment of the matter.

In a third picture God depicts his people in their *lethal divisions* (9:18-21). Wickedness consumes: 'Wickedness burns like fire' (v. 18a). But it's not as though wickedness is some impersonal power that can do that; it's really 'the fury of Yahweh of hosts' that scorches the land (v. 19a). And it's not as though 'the land' is the chief victim – 'the people have become like fuel for the fire' (v. 19b). They are set against one another and consume one another.

This Israel-versus-Israel note comes out clearly in verses 19c-21a. Customary human compassion has dried up: 'No one has pity on anyone else' (v. 19c). It's everyone for himself. All concern is turned inward on 'number one'. Verse 20 alludes to the frustration that folks under Yahweh's judgment meet (note: cut meat, remain famished; eat, not satisfied) – such aggravating futility is the way the covenant curses work (Deut. 28:20, 30, 38-40). In face of such frustration 'they eat the flesh of their own seed' (v. 20c).[5] This could refer to 'cannibalism' under siege conditions (cf. Deut. 28:52-57) or, as Gary Smith suggests, may simply refer in a metaphorical way to the rash of political assassinations in Israel (2 Kings 15). Then there are the inter-tribal conflicts: Manasseh versus Ephraim and vice versa – and when they do unite it is to combat their southern relative, Judah (v. 21a). This last may be a reference to the Syro-Ephraimite war (see our discussion in Isa. 7). Wickedness devours (v. 18), but it seems to do so by dividing (vv. 19c, 20c, 21a).

One still finds such division today among those who profess to be united. In June 1967, the Russians (then the U.S.S.R.) knew the exact date when Israel planned to strike Egypt, but they did not inform their ally. They had armed Egypt and the Arabs to the teeth and didn't want the Arabs defeated; but

---

5. The traditional Hebrew text reads 'their/his own arm'; I have opted to read the very similar (in Hebrew) 'seed' instead of 'arm' (cf. NIV).

they also wanted the war. They were somewhat dubious about Egypt's Nasser – if he knew the attack was coming he might back out and have his troops retreat from Sinai.[6] The 'solution' is not to tell your ally what is coming! Even in their unity there is division. That is what we see in verses 18-21: division – and ruin.

Finally, God depicts Israel in her *intentional injustice* (10:1-4). Nothing very discreet here. Rather blatant in fact, very deliberate. Those who have control of the legal machinery issue decrees that they can use to pad their own power and increase their own wealth. Perhaps they have their own staff of paralegals ('writers who write'), who draft laws and can finesse them in such a way that will enable these rulers to 'foreclose' on widows and so add to their own holdings. Interestingly, in verse 2b Yahweh refers to 'the afflicted of my people', which may imply that even in the apostasy-infected northern kingdom Yahweh still had a faithful, if abused, remnant. But these wheeler-dealers will find that they will face a 'day of punishment', a time of ruin, when escape will not be an option; no recourse will be open to them except to hunker down among those slated for deportation (10:4a) – or worse (10:4b, 'and they will fall where those killed fall'). So tragic to have all that carefully accumulated wealth and not know where to dump it (10:3d)!

The sketch in verses 3-4 brings to mind the decision Arthur Peuchen once had to make. He was a chemist from Toronto on a trans-Atlantic voyage. He stepped out of his first-class cabin one night clutching three oranges. You see, he was on the *Titanic*. He left behind a tin box containing $200,000 in bonds and $100,000 in preferred stock.[7] There are times when

---

6. Jacques Derogy and Hesi Carmel, *The Untold History of Israel* (New York: Grove Press, 1979), pp. 217-18.

7. Richard Bewes, *Words that Circled the World* (Ross-shire: Christian Focus, 2002), p. 15.

fruit trumps funds. These slick land-sharks of Israel will face a similar dilemma. Somehow wealth has little clout or use when one is simply another shivering captive waiting to experience the tender mercies of the Assyria Deportation Program.

So ... these are the people Yahweh depicts. But who is meant to look at and ponder these pictures? Probably not the people of the northern kingdom themselves. As Gary Smith suggests, we're probably not to imagine Isaiah wandering up to the northern kingdom to deliver these scenarios. More likely, 'Isaiah speaks to the Hebrew people *in Judah* about the consequences of Israel's sin.'[8] One might say Isaiah was using northern kingdom disasters as negative teaching models for southern kingdom folks.[9] It's something like a North American sports scenario. Let's say we're in college basketball and that Wake Forest has lost in miserable fashion to Duke. Now pretend Auburn was soon slated to play Duke and that the Auburn coach showed the film of the Wake Forest-Duke game to his players. He highlights the errors of the losing team: failure to 'block out' in rebounding, taking too many long, lower-percentage shots, hesitancy to drive to the basket and force fouls inside, and so on. His critique is not for the team Duke defeated but for his team who is about to face Duke. So with Isaiah: he sketches northern pictures for southern eyes. It's as if Yahweh says, 'Look at how I have decimated and will

---

8. Gary V. Smith, *Isaiah 1-39*, New American Commentary (Nashville: Broadman & Holman, 2007), p. 243 (emphasis mine).

9. One likely finds a similar pattern at work in the prophecies against the nations (Isa. 13–23). Not likely that Isaiah went to these various nations to deliver these messages nor that he slapped extra postage on them to get them out to such distant post codes. Rather, they were meant for local consumption in Judah, as if to say, 'Look, if all these nations are under Yahweh's judgment, why do you people of Judah pander after them for help? Why are you so impressed with such doomed entities?' See John N. Oswalt, *The Book of Isaiah, Chapters 1–39*, New International Commentary on the Old Testament (Grand Rapids: Eerdmans, 1986), pp. 298-99. See also Chisholm, p. 47.

decimate insolent, unrepentant Israel and take warning – or these pictures will depict you.'

It is not then that Judah can relax because these prophecies threaten Israel and have nothing to do with the southern kingdom. Mardy Grothe tells of the time after the death of England's Charles II in 1685. His Roman Catholic brother, James II, assumed the throne. The Duke of Monmouth (Charles II's son) led a rebellion against James II. This revolt was short-lived, the rebels were brought to 'justice' and that before 'Hanging Judge Jeffreys.' During the trial Judge Jeffreys stuck his cane into the chest of one of the rebels and exclaimed, 'There is a rogue at the end of my cane!' The defendant, doubtless knowing his case was hopeless anyway, replied with commendable spunk, 'At which end, my Lord?'[10] Perhaps Jeffreys had never considered that 'rogue' could apply to him. And the danger for Judah would be to think that all Isaiah's ink was only spilled to condemn the northern kingdom. One can't help but hear echoes of Jesus: 'Unless you repent, you will all likewise perish' (Luke 13:3, 5).

The second major division of our passage focuses on **the anger God brings**, underscored by the four-fold refrain, 'for all this his anger has not turned away but his hand is stretched out still' (9:12, 17, 21; and 10:4). The fury of Yahweh has already been on display in scourges that have already come (see 9:19), but this refrain is saying that we haven't seen anything yet. Yahweh's wrath is far from satisfied and there is more of it to come. Meeting no repentance on earth, the wrath of heaven will only get 'worse'.

We can sometimes misuse a repeated formula like this, for we may easily recognize it as a literary device and almost leave it at that – without ever asking what it actually means. But it surely functions as more than a marker for dividing the passage into appropriate 'chunks'. Each occurrence reminds

---

10. Mardy Grothe, *viva la repartee* (New York: Collins, 2005), p. 19.

us that 'more than this is coming', but there may be something climactic about the last occurrence in 10:4. In the first part of the verse Isaiah had pictured Israel's well-heeled oppressors as captives trying to make themselves invisible among other soon-to-be deportees *and* as ones who were apparently killed along with some of the other casualties. Then comes this 'for all this his anger has not turned away.' Is this implying that there is 'more anger' operating even beyond their deaths? Geoffrey Grogan drives this home:

> The refrain that has occurred at various points in this oracle is truly terrifying in its climactic position (v. 4b). If even physical death does not satisfy the fierce anger of this holy God, what dread punishment lies beyond the grave? No such device as this refrain is ever merely formal when it occurs in the Word of God.[11]

Reading Grogan is very much like listening to Jesus:

> I tell you, my friends, do not fear those who kill the body, and after that have nothing more that they can do. But I will warn you whom to fear: fear him who, after he has killed, has authority to cast into hell. Yes, I tell you, fear him! (Luke 12:4-5, esv).

There is a sense in which we should be frightened of death – that should have been so in eighth century Israel. One might hope Israel would get the point of Yahweh's preliminary samples of his anger. This, however, was not happening: 'But the people have not turned back to the One who struck them' (9:13). Hence 'his anger has not turned away' and his hand will be 'stretched out still' – all the way to perdition. If Israel is dense, we should not be about Whom to fear.

---

11. Geoffrey W. Grogan, 'Isaiah,' in *The Expositor's Bible Commentary*, rev. ed., 13 vols. (Grand Rapids: Zondervan, 2008), 6:534.

HOW THEY STRUT,
HOW THEY FALL!
(Isaiah 10:5-34)

(5)   Woe to Assyria,
      rod of my anger!
      And my rage is the staff in their hands.

(6)   Against a godless nation I will send him
      and against the people of my fury I will order him,
      to scoop up spoil
      and to pilfer plunder
      and to make him a stomping-ground like street mud.

(7)   But he will not plan (it) like that,
      and his heart will not think like that,
      but annihilation is in his heart
      and cutting off nations
      – (and) not merely a few (of them).

(8)   For he says,
      'Are not my commanders all kings?

(9)   Will not Calno prove like Carchemish?
      Or will not Hamath be like Arpad?
      Or will not Samaria be like Damascus?

(10) As my hand has reached to the kingdoms
            of worthless deities
      and their carved images were more numerous
            than those of Jerusalem and Samaria,

(11) as I have done to Samaria and her non-gods,
      will I not do to Jerusalem and to her idols?'

(12) And it shall be
      when the Lord finishes up his work
            in Mt. Zion and in Jerusalem,
      I will punish the fruit of the massive arrogance
            of the king of Assyria
            and his high and mighty look.

(13) For he has said,
      'By the power of my hand I have done (it)
      and by my wisdom, for I am discerning,
      and I took away the boundaries of peoples
      and their treasures I have plundered,
      and like a bull I brought down those who sit
            (on thrones);

(14) and my hand found, like (finding) a nest,
            the wealth of the peoples
      and like gathering abandoned eggs
            I have gathered **all the earth**,
      and there's not been anyone moving a wing
            or opening a mouth
            – not (even) a peep.'

(15) Should the axe boast against the one who whacks
            with it?

Or should the saw magnify itself against the one
    using it?
Like a rod controlling the one who lifts it up!
Like a staff lifting up someone who's
    not wood!

(16) Therefore the Lord, Yahweh of hosts,
        will send leanness among his fat ones,
    and under his glory
        a burning will burn like a burning of fire.

(17) And the Light of Israel shall become a fire
        and his Holy One a flame,
    and it shall burn and consume his briers
        and his thorn-bushes in one day;

(18) and the glory of his forest and of his garden-land
        – from soul to body—he will finish off,
    and it shall be like a sick man wasting away.

(19) And the remnant of the trees of his forest
        will be (so) few that a lad can write them down.

(20) And it shall be on that day
    that the remnant of Israel and the escapees
        of the house of Jacob
    will no longer lean on him who struck them down
    but they will lean upon Yahweh, the Holy One of Israel,
        in faithfulness.

(21) A remnant will return,
    a remnant of Jacob, to El Gibbor [the mighty God].

(22) Though your people, O Israel, may be
        like the sand of the sea,
    a **remnant** of it will return;
    annihilation is decreed,
        overflowing with righteousness.

(23) For a full and decisive end the Lord, Yahweh of hosts,

is going to make
in the midst of all the earth.

(24) Therefore, here's what the Lord, Yahweh of hosts, says,
'Do not fear, my people,
who dwell in Zion,
(do not fear) Assyria —
he strikes you with the rod
and lifts up his staff over you the way Egypt did.

(25) For yet a very little while
and my rage shall come to an end
and my anger (will bring about) their destruction.

(26) And Yahweh of hosts shall stir up a whip against him,
as when he struck down Midian at the rock of Oreb,
and his staff will be over the sea
and he shall lift it up as in Egypt.

(27) And it shall be on that day
his burden will depart from your shoulder
and his yoke from your neck,
and (the) yoke shall be destroyed because of fatness.'

(28) He has come to Aiath;
he has passed through Migron;
at Michmash he stashes his baggage.

(29) They have passed through the pass!
'Geba will be our stop for the night.'
Ramah trembles;
Gibeah of Saul has fled.

(30) Scream, daughters of Gallim!
Pay attention, Laishah!
Poor Anathoth!

(31) Madmenah has fluttered off;
the residents of Gebim seek safety (elsewhere).

(32) Yet today he stands at Nob;
    he shakes his fist at the mountain of Daughter Zion,
        at the hill of Jerusalem.

(33) Look! The Lord, Yahweh of hosts, is going to chop off
        branches with an awful crash
    and the high ones will get whacked down
    and the tall ones will be brought low;

(34) and he shall cut down the forest thickets with an axe,
    and Lebanon will fall because of the Majestic One.

Early in our marriage my wife and I were back visiting her home church in rural western Kansas. During morning worship that Sunday one of the church men gave the 'children's sermon'. He told the kids about 'the Lord's rooster', a cock on the farm that apparently knew he had been somehow dedicated to the Lord and so because of that strutted and swaggered around, well, cockily. Yes sir, he was no common chicken; he was a cut above – he was *the Lord's* rooster. I confess I cannot now conjure up all the details, but I believe it turned out that he was dubbed the Lord's rooster because his owners had committed him for a special purpose – something like being roasted for a church repast. That's enough to take the fluff out of your feathers and put some congestion in your crow. And, of course, nations can become like roosters, especially if they happen to increase in power, enjoy some success, and are able to dominate other nations. They begin to think they just may be the top cock in God's barnyard and may not realize that his anger, that has not turned away from his people, might strike them as well (cf. 10:4). God's covenant people throughout the world need to remember this – need to 're-realize' that our God is not merely over a few Christian ghettos scattered across the globe but that he is Lord of the nations. He is not just in charge of *covenant* matters but of *cosmic* matters. Yahweh sees that nations who strut also fall.

I don't assume that you are dying to hear more about Assyria, but suffice to say that from about the time Tiglath-pileser III (= Pul) seized the Assyrian throne in 745 B.C., Assyria experienced a resurgence that made it the big military machine and super-power of the day. Assyria enjoyed such dominance through the reigns of Tiglath-pileser III (745–727), Shalmaneser V (726–722), Sargon II (721–705), and Sennacherib (705–681).[1] In the 730s B.C. Ahaz of Judah had appealed to Tiglath-pileser for relief, because Judah was getting creamed by Philistines and Edomites as well as by Syria and Israel. Ahaz preferred Assyrian power to Yahweh's promise. Since Ahaz wanted Assyrians, Yahweh would see that he got them – with a vengeance (7:17-20). Verse 12 of our present text sums up Yahweh's activity in all this: Yahweh is using Assyria to carry out his work 'in Mt. Zion and in Jerusalem', and, when he finishes that work, he will cut Assyria down to size.

This 'woe' (v. 5) against Assyria is for Judah's ears. And, if we expand the scope of the text beyond Assyria alone, we could summarize it like this: *The Lord of the church is the ruler of nations, and while ruling the nations he never forgets his church.* Let's develop this under the heads of several principles.

The Lord uses nations as the instruments of his judgment (vv. 5-7).

Immediately we run into God's strange servants (vv. 5-6). The Assyrians are the 'rod of [Yahweh's] anger', his rage, he says, is 'the staff in their hands' (v. 5). Yahweh 'sends' them against his own people Judah, a people he calls 'a godless nation' (v. 6a). Profane Assyria is Yahweh's apostle against 'the people of my fury', as the super-power carries out Yahweh's judgment on

---

1. See further, Sandra Richter, 'Eighth-Century Issues,' in *Ancient Israel's History*, ed. Bill T. Arnold and Richard S. Hess (Grand Rapids: Baker, 2014), pp. 337-42.

Judah. They are the Lord's executioners.[2] Of course, Assyria does not know this, probably wouldn't believe it if they were told.[3] They are attacking and threatening and conquering to plunder and destroy and dominate. Yet Yahweh is using what Assyria freely desires to do to fulfill his own sovereign design against Judah.

The Assyrians, however, are not only God's strange servants but his restive servants (v. 7). They are not thinking like Yahweh is. They don't see themselves as functioning within the limited confines of Yahweh's purposes. They are going after the jugular: 'but annihilation is in his heart and cutting off nations – (and) not merely a few (of them)' (v. 7b). Their lust for conquest knows no bounds; they plan to run over and crush everything/one in their path. Their arrogance would step over the lines Yahweh has drawn. They want to go too far.

That brings on trouble. Ask Arthur Furguson. He was a dapper, diminutive Scotsman with a charming manner who came to the U.S.A. in 1925 since Scotland Yard was hot on his heels in Britain. In Washington, he posed as a government official and managed to lease the White House to a cattle rancher for $100,000 per year. The first yearly payment was, naturally, due in advance. His line was that they were going to build another presidential residence and fees for tours of the 'old,' leased White House would cover the cost of the lease. With a bag full of money Furguson vamoosed to New York, planning to go straight. But there was an Australian tourist beside him as they both stood admiring the Statue of Liberty. He couldn't resist. Yes, it was too bad, he averred:

---

2. See, similarly, Habakkuk 1:6, where however Babylon is Yahweh's scourge against Judah.

3. The Assyrian statement in 2 Kings 18:25 is creative propaganda not heart-felt conviction.

they were having to sell and move the statuesque lady because they needed to widen the harbor for ships. And he, as a highly placed government official had the unpleasant task of finding a buyer. Did you ask how much? One hundred thousand. Furguson grew nervous over the several days the Australian was trying to conjure up the funds from friends back in Sydney. Finally, the 'buyer' grew suspicious, told the police, and finished Furguson's folly.[4] Assyria is like that – simply won't lay aside her insatiable lust for 'more'. Assyria preens herself as 'conqueror'; Yahweh looks on her as 'servant', the 'rod of my anger.'

We don't have the light of direct revelation today to know how Yahweh may be using nations in what seems to be the ongoing crises and jumbled chaos of our world. But if hairy-chested Assyria was once his servant to do his will, then surely he has not abandoned his sovereign rule of men and nations.

Assyria's attitude in verse 7 pushes us toward our next principle: **The Lord punishes nations for their arrogant self-deification** (vv. 8-19, 28-34). The problem is that the rod of Yahweh's anger thinks he is a hot rod. The Assyrian's program is to show that he has the biggest biceps in the middle east.

The first matter we should notice is that the arrogance of Assyria *is* an impressive arrogance. Notice the 'quotations' Isaiah puts into the Assyrian's mouth in, for example, verse 9:

> Will not Calno prove like Carchemish?
> Or will not Hamath be like Arpad?
> Or will not Samaria be like Damascus?[5]

---

4. Thomas Ayres, *That's Not in My American History Book* (Lanham, MD: Taylor Trade, 2004), pp. 122-23.

5. For this translation and sense of the text, see Alec Motyer, *The Prophecy of Isaiah* (Downers Grove, IL: Inter-Varsity, 1993), p. 114, and Gary V. Smith, *Isaiah 1–39*, New American Commentary (Nashville: Broadman & Holman, 2007), pp. 253, 257.

This is Assyrian logic. Carchemish sits on the upper Euphrates about 100 miles east of the N.E. corner of the Mediterranean Sea. In the ninth and eighth centuries Assyrian rulers conquered and plundered it almost at will.[6] Wouldn't Calno (perhaps sixty miles S.W. of Carchemish) prove Act II of Carchemish? In 738 it did. Or there's Arpad (also S.W. of Carchemish), conquered and made an Assyrian province by Tiglath-pileser III ca. 740 B.C. And in 738 Hamath (120 miles N./N.E. of Damascus) had to surrender a huge amount of turf to Assyria, until 720 when Assyria absorbed all of it into her empire.[7] And in 722 Samaria did become like Damascus in 732. None of the 'worthless deities' (v. 10) could protect their devotees from Assyria's power, and surely he will knock off Jerusalem (Yes, his eyes are on her!) just as he did Samaria (v. 11). It looks like an air-tight case. We shouldn't think of one specific Assyrian king saying all this. It is a collage. It's an Assyrian *attitude*. As if he says, 'I can simply roll over the world.' And his words in verses 13-14 simply reinforce this: his repeated 'I … I … I …' incarnates his inflated ego, while the imagery ('like gathering abandoned eggs,' v. 14) depicts how easily he conquers and pilfers. And no one has the gall to object (v. 14b).

This boasting seems largely accurate. Assyria often tried to get cities to submit without the cost of a siege or combat. Should cities prove recalcitrant, the Assyrians might choose a smaller city to attack, one they could take easily, and then commit 'extreme acts of cruelty' to show what happened to folks who didn't submit peacefully. Though he's pre-Isaiah by over a hundred years Ashurnasirpal II (885–860) gives a taste of the 'Assyrian way':

---

6. R. Youngblood, ISBE, 1:616. Hence the reference here need not be to Sargon's destruction of it as late as 717.

7. M-L. Buhl, 'Hamath,' ABD, 3:34.

In strife and conflict I besieged (and) conquered the city. I felled 3,000 of their fighting men with the sword. I carried off prisoners, possessions, oxen, (and) cattle from them. I burnt many captives from them. I captured many troops alive: I cut off of some their arms (and) hands; I cut off of others their noses, ears, (and) extremities. I gouged out the eyes of many troops. I made one pile of the living (and) one of the heads. I hung their heads on trees around the city. I burnt their adolescent boys (and) girls. I razed, destroyed, burnt, (and) consumed the city.[8]

After such displays other cities suddenly became docile.

If, however, Assyrian arrogance is impressive, it is also absurd (v. 15), for this insolence is met with news of her coming demise (vv. 16-19). One senses an undertone of mockery in the quotations of verses 8-11 and 13-14. But the disdain explodes off the page in verse 15. It's as if Isaiah (and/or Yahweh) gags in unbelief: Can you be serious?

> Should the axe boast against the one who whacks with it?
> Or should the saw magnify itself against the one using it?
> Like a rod controlling the one who lifts it up!
> Like a staff lifting up someone who's not wood!

The Assyrian does not realize he is a tool, an instrument, to be used by Another. The real 'work' going on is not Assyria's empire but Yahweh's purpose, and when he finishes that (v. 12a), he will put Assyria in her place (v. 12b). He gives two pictures of Assyria's demise: a sudden inferno, like flames consuming dry briers and thorn-bushes (vv. 16-17) and a gradual decay, like a ravaging sickness that wastes a man away (v. 18). One can see part of the fulfillment of these verses (i.e., vv. 16-19) in 37:36-37. So much for the big red machine that thought it could wipe out the hick nations of the world.

---

8. A. Kirk Grayson, 'Assyrian Rule of Conquered Territory in Ancient Western Asia,' in *Civilizations of the Ancient Near East*, ed. Jack M. Sasson, 4 vols. (New York: Charles Scribner's Sons, 1995), 2:961.

Verses 28-34 also depict Assyria's demise by means of what we might call a parting cartoon – or perhaps we should limit the 'cartoon' to verses 33-34. At any rate, Isaiah sketches the north-to-south advance of an enemy (think: Assyria) on Jerusalem, inciting terror and panic in all who are in its path,[9] and sympathy from the prophet (cf. v. 30). Isaiah portrays the enemy as invincible (vv. 28-31), then frustrated (v. 32), and finally destroyed (vv. 33-34). The 'cartoon' appears in these two final verses: there is Yahweh, the divine lumberjack, chopping and whacking down the forest of towering trees labeled 'Assyria'. So, the Lord punishes nations for their arrogant self-deification.

Deity-complexes are horribly easy to come by. One doesn't have to be an outstanding individual nor a particularly powerful nation to get one. Think of May 9, 1936. After his troops had crushed a largely defenseless Abyssinia (Ethiopia), Mussolini stood in a balcony overlooking the Piazza Venezia and boasted to thousands that Italy at last had her empire – a Fascist Empire. Mussolini had defied the League of Nations and had frustrated Hitler himself, whose agents had supplied the Abyssinians with limited arms. He stood, without movement or expression, looking out over the sea of his devotees, basking in the adulation of thousands chanting 'Duce, Duce, Duce.' The crowd recalled him to the balcony forty-two times. The strut was there. But

---

9. Some think Isaiah portrays Sennacherib's threat on Jerusalem in 701 B.C. One can't be sure. Sennacherib's henchmen and forces likely approached Jerusalem from the west/southwest, from Lachish and Libnah (see Isa. 36-37) instead of from the north as here. Some seem to think Isaiah is giving an 'idealized' (we could say picture-fied) description of such an enemy's relentless approach, one not tied to any historical occurrence (cf. Oswalt), or perhaps there could have been two contingents of Assyrian forces in 701, one from the west/southwest, another from the north (cf. graphics in *Macmillan Bible Atlas*, 3rd ed., p. 118), or perhaps Sennacherib's force made a circuit around to the north instead of proceeding in from the west (so G. W. Grogan, 'Isaiah,' *Expositor's Bible Commentary*, rev. ed., 13 vols. [Grand Rapids: Zondervan, 2008], 6:542).

six years later, about July 1942, after a disastrous trip to North Africa, his wife would see him rolling on the floor, in agony as he clutched his stomach. This intestinal trouble peeled fifty pounds off him. One specialist brought in to assist in his care remarked, 'What is he, after all? Just a failed journalist with ulcers.' And about three years later that failed journalist would be hanging by his feet, along with his mistress, from the girders of a bombed-out service station in Milan.[10]

Powerful nations stand on tenuous ground. A text like this should induce a sober attitude in the super-powers of our day. But, of course, it won't. No nation wants to hear this or will hear it, and I doubt there is any contemporary nation whose government really believes there is a God who sovereignly rules, directs, and judges men and nations. I live in a nation that is often dubbed a 'super-power'. And I cringe, especially in election years, when various politicians speak of our country as 'the most powerful nation in the world'. Really? And yet we haven't won a war in how many years? Could it be that Yahweh is telling us something?

I like the story of the time young Franklin Roosevelt, while Assistant Secretary of the Navy, was visiting Henry Adams in the latter's study on Lafayette Square. FDR was going on about the Wilson administration and Adams shushed him, and said: 'Young man, I have lived in this house many years and seen the occupants of that White House across the square come and go, and nothing that you minor officials or the occupants of that house can do will affect the history of the world for long!'[11] Perhaps overly-cynical but salutary nonetheless. Not said to a nation but only to a government official – yet it's the sort of blow to our deity-complexes that we need. Nations especially.

---

10. See Richard Collier, *Duce!* (New York: Viking, 1971), pp. 128-32, 184-85.

11. Joseph P. Lash, *Eleanor and Franklin* (New York: W. W. Norton, 1971), p. 189.

Otherwise, nations can, too late, find themselves in Ezekiel 32 – sitting next to Assyria in Sheol.

Now, a final principle: **The Lord's work among the nations is always directed toward the benefit of his church** (vv. 20-27). We have two chunks of text in this section, verses 20-23 and 24-27. We meet 'on that day' at the beginning in verse 20 and 'in that day' at the beginning of verse 27 at the end of the section. This 'day' is not primarily the final 'day' but primarily the day of Yahweh's deliverance from Assyria.

Although it may seem pedantic, I think we can summarize the teaching of these verses in three propositions. The first is: *Yahweh refines his church* (v. 20). As verse 20 now sits, 'that day' (v. 20a) harks back to verses 16-19, the day when Yahweh finishes off Assyria. Time was when Judah under Ahaz had leaned upon Assyria as the solution to her multi-faceted troubles (cf. 2 Kings 16:7, and our previous discussion of Isa. 7), but time would come when those who survived would see that far from being a cozy savior Assyria had proven a cruel opponent (Isa. 7:17-25; 36:1ff.), one 'who struck them down' (v. 20b), and, like King Hezekiah (37:14-20), they would find they must rest upon Yahweh alone. Yahweh will teach his people that they must only lean on the everlasting arms.

And, further, *Yahweh preserves his church* (vv. 21-23). Isaiah seems to play off the name of his older son, Shear-jashub ('a remnant will return'; cf. 7:3) again. He seems to stress both 'sides' of the name. 'A remnant will return' (v. 21a), but the return is not geographical but penitential: they will return 'to the mighty God' (El Gibbor; cf. 9:6). Here then is a *repentant* people who will lean upon Yahweh (a la verse 20c). And yet it seems *only* a remnant will return: 'Though your people, O Israel, may be like the sand of the sea [cf. Gen. 22:17], a remnant [emphatic] of it will return' (v. 22a). Whatever one makes of the details, these verses are telling us that in face of the coming, ordained, righteous, consuming judgment, Yahweh is going to preserve a repentant remnant as his own.[12] Yahweh simply refuses to allow a faithful people to be extinguished.

Finally, we see that *Yahweh relieves his church* (vv. 24-27). Here Yahweh addresses his people who are – or will be – enduring the ravages of Assyria (v. 24). These verses may point to the assault of Sennacherib on King Hezekiah and Judah ca. 701 B.C. Sennacherib boasts of the ruin he inflicted in his annals:

> But as for Hezekiah, the Jew, who did not bow in submission to my yoke, forty-six of his strong walled towns and innumerable smaller villages in their neighbourhood I besieged and conquered by stamping down earth-ramps and then by bringing up battering rams, by the assault of foot-soldiers, by breaches, tunnelling and sapper operations. I made to come out from them 200,150 people, young and old, male and female, innumerable horses, mules, donkeys, camels, large and small cattle, and counted them as the spoils of war. He himself I shut up like a caged bird within Jerusalem, his royal city.[13]

Isaiah 1:7-9 may describe these very conditions. But in 'a very little while' (v. 25a) Yahweh's anger will be turned to Assyria's destruction (v. 25c). Yahweh will reprise his victories over Midian (v. 26a; cf. Judg. 7:24-25) and over Egypt (v. 26b), all of which will spell freedom for his people (v. 27).[14] And so he did

---

12. Note that Paul cites 10:22-23 in Romans 9:27-28.

13. D. Winton Thomas, ed., *Documents from Old Testament Times* (New York: Harper & Row, 1958), p. 67.

14. Verse 27 is clear enough even if the last clause is obscure. Note that in v. 24 Assyria will oppress the way Egypt did, and in v. 26 Yahweh will deliver as he did in Egypt. J. Ridderbos nicely combines these two references: 'Just as Assyria oppresses Israel, Egyptian-style (v. 24), so it will be destroyed, Egyptian-style, when at the word of the Lord the waters of destruction will cover it' (*Isaiah*, Bible Student's Commentary [Grand Rapids: Zondervan, 1985], p. 119).

– see 37:36-37. The army surplus stores in Judah were selling thousands of used Assyrian sleeping bags dirt cheap. What welcome words then:

> Do not fear, my people,
> who dwell in Zion,
> do not fear Assyria ….
> For yet a very little while …
> And my anger will bring about his destruction (vv. 24-25).

I think it is important to see that this liberation Yahweh promises is not the final or ultimate deliverance of the last day. Clearly, this is a deliverance in the midst of history. Yahweh will not only save his people at the last but often saves them along the way. He relieves them in their dire emergencies, in their desolate circumstances along the time-line on the way to Messiah's final kingdom. Where would we be if Yahweh did not stoop down and periodically remove the yoke from the neck of his beleaguered Zion?

One thinks of that day in early November 1688 when William of Orange landed on the shores of England, so that James II 'found it politic to slip quietly out of England and spend Christmas on the continent'.[15] And what did that mean for the church in Scotland? It meant the end of the tyranny and absolutism of James and his lackeys. It meant the end of twenty-eight years of relentless persecution; it meant that 'the killing times' had expired; it meant that faithful ministers and saints would no longer be hounded, harassed, hunted, and hung. No longer would they be imprisoned, exiled, tortured, murdered, raped, and pillaged. Does that mean that everyone was completely happy with the 'revolution settlement' under William and Mary or that all such conditions were ideal? No, but Yahweh had lifted the yoke; the Lord Christ had looked

---

15. J. D. Douglas, *Light in the North* (Grand Rapids: Eerdmans, 1964), p. 175.

with pity on his remnant and brought them relief. Relief, lest they be totally crushed.

Yahweh's arm may be establishing or eliminating nations, but his eye is always on his Zion, who is ever pitied, protected, and provided for.[16] The Lord of the church is the ruler of nations, and while ruling the nations he never forgets his church.

---

16. cf. The Westminster Confession of Faith, chapter 12.

7 THE STUMP KINGDOM
(Isaiah 11)

(1) And a twig shall come forth from the stump of Jesse,
and a shoot from his roots will bear fruit.

(2) And the Spirit of Yahweh shall rest upon him—
the Spirit of wisdom and understanding,
the Spirit of counsel and might,
the Spirit of knowledge and of the fear of Yahweh.

(3) And his delight will be in the fear of Yahweh;
and he will not judge merely by what his eyes see,
and he will not decide cases merely by what his ears hear,

(4) but with righteousness he shall judge the helpless,
and in uprightness he shall decide for the afflicted
of the earth;
and he shall smite the earth with the rod of his mouth,

and with the breath of his lips he will put the wicked
to death.

(5)   And righteousness shall be the belt around his waist
and faithfulness the belt around his mid-section.

(6)   And the wolf shall stay with the lamb;
and the leopard will stretch out with the young goat;
and the calf and the young lion and the head of
fattened cattle are together as well;
and a small lad will be leading them;

(7)   and the cow and the bear will graze—
their young ones will stretch out together;
and the lion will eat fodder like the ox;

(8)   and the nursing child shall play over the hole of the
serpent,
and the toddler shall stretch his hand over the den of
the snake.

(9)   They will not harm or bring ruin in all my holy mountain,
for the earth shall be filled with knowing Yahweh as the
waters cover the sea.

(10) And it shall be in that day –
the root of Jesse will be standing as a banner to the
peoples;
he is the one the nations will come seeking;
and his residence shall be sheer glory.

(11) And it shall be in that day—
the Lord will reach his hand out a second time to
acquire the remnant of his people,
who remain from Assyria and Egypt
and from Upper Egypt and Ethiopia
and Elam and Babylonia
and Hamath and the islands of the sea.

(12) And he shall raise a banner for the nations,
and he shall gather the outcasts of Israel,

and he will assemble the scattered ones of Judah
    from the four corners of the earth.

(13) And the jealousy of Ephraim shall depart,
    and the hostilities of Judah will be cut off;
    Ephraim will not be jealous of Judah,
    and Judah will not harass Ephraim.

(14) And they shall fly upon the shoulder of the Philistines
        to the west;
    together they will plunder the sons of the east;
    their hand will control Edom and Moab,
    and the sons of Ammon will be their subjects.

(15) And Yahweh shall destroy the tongue of the sea
        of Egypt,
    and he shall wave his hand over the River (Euphrates)
        with his scorching wind,
    and he shall smite it into seven channels
    so that people can cross it with their sandals on.

(16) And there shall be a highway for the remnant of
        his people
        who remain from Assyria,
    just as there was for Israel on the day they came up
        from the land of Egypt.[1]

Hard to know the date for the message of Isaiah 11 – perhaps it
came during the prophet's go-round with Ahaz in the 730s, or
perhaps it was given some years later in Hezekiah's reign (see
Isa. 36-37), when Assyria still seemed to be thriving as the 'rod'

---

1. Note on the translation: The reader may note how repeatedly the conjunction 'and' occurs in my translation. That's because it's in the text and,
though it lacks in style, I want the reader to feel the 'piling up' effect of one
detail upon another as Isaiah describes the messianic reign. This is especially the case as one reads verses 1-9 – you feel like you've been dumped
down in the Second Gospel and Mark pulls you along at a breathless pace
with his seemingly unending conjunctions: 'and... and... and....' So here;
Isaiah probably intends for your heart rate to increase as you read.

of God's anger (cf. 10:5). Imagine the latter. Let's be anachronistic and more, and pretend it's Christmas time in 701 B.C. in Judah and Jerusalem.

Well, it's a good bit different from Christmas in 702 B.C. The rainy drizzle is the same but there's no 'Silver Bells' blasting out of municipal loudspeakers. No one in Moishe's Appliances is buying flat screen TVs or microwaves, even though Moishe has drastically discounted the whole lot. Benjamin's Bar and Grill is full – some folks are boozing themselves silly. The Farmers' Market is crowded – folks grabbing up what wheat, barley, cereal, and fruit they can. No one watches the Christmas specials on TV – they're all tuned to the 24-hour news channels where they can watch the clips about how the Assyrian army has surrounded the city and hear excerpts of the verbal gas its commander was feeding the king's cabinet officers. The 'warfare' is psychological at the moment; it could be physical soon enough. No one from the Lions Club was selling cedar trees this year.

A bit imaginative. But the time came when Assyria and Sennacherib were choking Judah within an inch of its life (cf. 1:7-9). If we can believe Sennacherib's propaganda, he had taken forty-six walled towns and over 200,000 captives. David's kingdom – currently Hezekiah's kingdom – was nearly whacked down to a stump, and Isaiah proclaims the coming of the Messiah. The testimony of the text seems to be: *The messianic King is your only hope and you should long voraciously for his rule.* What particularly does the prophet want us to see?

He wants us to see, first of all, **how hopeless God's kingdom looks** (vv. 1, 10):

> And a twig shall come forth from the stump of Jesse,
> and a shoot from his roots will bear fruit (v. 1).

The 'And' is really there in the text. It shows the material in chapter 11 is actually connected with what's in 10:5-34. If Yahweh is going to wallop the arrogant Assyrian 'tree' down to nothing

(10:33-34), we must also remember that there will be something else that looks like nothing – the Davidic kingdom itself (11:1).

Let's try to take in the picture. Isaiah takes us back not merely to David but to 'the stump of Jesse'. David was the one who arose from Jesse and so the 'twig' and 'shoot' from Jesse's stump and roots will be a new 'David'.[2] But the royal line will seem to be nothing but a stump. Stumps don't look promising. The 'stump' points to what is desolate, defunct, and demolished. And yet strange things can happen around stumps. In our last pastorate in southern Mississippi there was a tree that was getting too big for its britches. It was flourishing too well and its branches were invading one space in the church parking lot and making it almost unusable. But after some time of suffering inconvenience, apparently an angel with a chainsaw took down this small-to-medium sized nuisance. I thought it had been done on the Deacons' orders, but, as it turned out, the 'angel' was an unauthorized one. In any case, we now had, happily, nothing but a stump there. But ere long a sprig, a shoot, came up beside that stump. Stumps image desolation but harbor life. And Isaiah indicates that the Messiah will arise at a time when the nation and kingdom look pretty pathetic and powerless.

But not hopeless. It is not hopeless because the shoot of Jesse is also the root of Jesse, as per verse 10:

> And it shall be in that day—
> the root of Jesse will be standing as a banner to the peoples;
> he is the one the nations will come seeking … .

I don't think we should tone this down. I think Isaiah is deliberately playing on the 'shoot and root' paradox. The 'root of Jesse' is an image implying that this one is also the source and origin of Jesse.[3] And yet the 'root of Jesse' is also a title,

---

2. 'The reference to *Jesse* indicates that the *shoot* is not just another king in David's line but rather another David' (J. A. Motyer, *The Prophecy of Isaiah* [Downers Grove, IL: Inter-Varsity, 1993], p. 121).

3. See, Motyer, p. 121.

and a title for a person whom the nations will come seeking. It seems to me that the shoot-root conundrum points to both the human and divine nature of the Messiah. On the one hand he is the seed of Jesse, but on the other he is the *source* of Jesse; he is his offspring (twig, shoot) but also his *origin*. Perhaps you think it only a hint, but it looks like we are dealing with far more than simply a human Messiah here. Should it really surprise us, when Isaiah has already told us his name is Immanuel (ch. 7) and *El-gibbor* (ch. 9)? How often must he pound it into us?

Still it is a bleak picture. Judah and its kings will be whacked down to stumpdom (cf. 6:11-13). It will look as if the whole Israel game is over. How unlikely God's kingdom frequently looks. As Jesus indicated, it is often simply unimpressive, seems very mustard-seedy and about as visible as hidden leaven. And such appearances can be dismaying.

I remember seeing a car in our area of northeast Baltimore some years ago. It was a station wagon model, and a fairly substantial one, a Buick or an Oldsmobile. It was not a late model and the owner had lathered the rear bumper and tailgate with a plethora of stickers. In all the verbal litter, however, there was one sticker that was very clear, in the lower, left-hand corner of the tailgate, I believe. It read: This is *not* an abandoned car. The wisdom of that sticker was obvious, because it did look precisely like that. And Isaiah is doing something like that in verse 1: God's kingdom will look like an abandoned kingdom, but it will be in such circumstances that the messianic twig will appear. This is, of course, vintage Yahweh. God begins (or renews) his work in hopelessness and ruin and helplessness and weakness. But you don't have to supply him with a restoration-booster kit. He's accustomed to starting there.

Secondly, Isaiah wants you to see **how adequate God's Messiah is** (vv. 2-5). He speaks first of the Messiah's *equipping* by the Spirit of Yahweh (vv. 2-3a). He describes the Spirit of Yahweh in three lines and his gifts in three 'pairs'. The king will have the Spirit as the Spirit of 'wisdom and understanding', that is, wisdom but also the ability to use that wisdom in isolating and selecting the right option to follow; in a word, discernment. 'Counsel and might' implies the ability not only to form suitable plans but also having the power ('might') to put such plans into effect. Having the Spirit of 'knowledge and of the fear of Yahweh' implies that this king intimately knows Yahweh and is driven by a reverence-charged faithfulness to him. God's Spirit equips God's king to fulfill God's call. Verse 3a is difficult but seems to suggest that the messianic king himself delights in the relation and task for which the Spirit equips him; that is, he feels real 'gusto' for it.[4]

What effect then does the Spirit's equipping have on the rule of the messianic king? For one thing, he will rule in *truth*: 'and he will not judge merely by what his eyes see, and he will not decide cases merely by what his ears hear' (v. 3b). His discernment goes beyond the apparent and superficial, gets down below the veneer and spin-coating, and decides matters with uncanny accuracy. This sort of description (in v. 3b) 'appears again to be a reference to a more than merely human character possessed by the Messiah'.[5]

But even more so, he will rule in *justice*: 'but with righteousness he shall judge the helpless, and in uprightness he shall decide for the afflicted of the earth' (v. 4a). Here is a king who rightly puts things right. The 'helpless' and 'afflicted' are singled out as the particular beneficiaries of the Messiah's reign. Leupold puts it nicely:

> If they get their rights, every one else surely will. For that is the acid test of impartial administration of duties, not to overlook

---

4. cf. John L. MacKay, *a Study Commentary on Isaiah*, 2 vols. (Darlington: Evangelical Press, 2008), 1:292-93.

5. John N. Oswalt, *The Book of Isaiah: Chapters 1-39*, New International Commentary on the Old Testament (Grand Rapids: Eerdmans, 1986), p. 280.

the unimportant people. But this ruler has a heart for them and will champion their cause.[6]

And this is no mere ideal – the king has the 'Spirit of counsel *and might*' and so is able to enforce his just rule because he reigns with *power*:

> [A]nd he shall smite the earth
> with the rod of his mouth,
> and with the breath of his lips
> he will put the wicked to death (v. 4b).

This shows 'that Christ will never be without enemies, who will endeavor to overturn his kingdom' (Calvin), but he will not dally with them but by his mighty decree take them out of the way. His is no paper kingdom, no empty ideal – he enforces and imposes his program.

How welcome his reign will be, anchored as it is in righteousness and faithfulness (cf. v. 5). Only this morning I was reading in a prayer guide I use. It tells of a Pakistani Christian who was beaten to death by police four months ago after having been stripped naked and hung up until his shoulders were dislocated. He was for eighteen years a driver for a Muslim politician. His employer's wife accused him of stealing jewelry. So what do you do? Oh, you torture him and beat him to death in the police station on the 'testimony' of one witness. Or there are two Christian girls, twenty-one and twenty, sisters. They are kidnapped by Muslims about six months or so ago, forcibly converted to Islam, and forced to marry their kidnappers. One of them has managed to escape. But no return to family, for they themselves are under scrutiny and in danger. So lives are wrecked and ruined and futures shattered and no one is brought to justice. It happens about 700 times a year to Christian girls and women in Pakistan. Their

---

6. H. C. Leupold, *Exposition of Isaiah: Volume I, Chapters 1-39* (Grand Rapids: Baker, 1968), p. 219.

pillows (if they have them) are drenched in tears, the earth (or the floor of police stations) is wet with their blood – how they will welcome the One who will judge the helpless with righteousness and take up the cudgels for the afflicted of the earth!

So, there is this specific point that Christ's suffering people will especially welcome his reign. However, there is also a more general point to keep in view. Standing back and taking in the whole description of Christ's equipping and work in verses 2-5 should lead all believers to see how *satisfying* he is in every way. 'How fully this king meets our needs!' should be our response to the text. There is no deficiency in him; there is no disappointment in him. Isaiah wants to impress you with how adequate God's Messiah is.

I was recently re-reading Arthur John Gossip's (1873–1954) classic sermon, 'But When Life Tumbles in, What Then?' Dr Gossip preached the sermon not long after the sudden death of his wife. In view of that trial he said, 'I do not think that any one will challenge my right to speak today.' And what did he have to say? Well, he alluded to that horrid affair during the 'killing times' in Scotland, particularly to that incident in 1684 when the brute Claverhouse blew out the brains of John Brown of Priesthill at his cottage door, in front of his wife and bairns. Then Claverhouse turns to Isabel Brown and asks: 'What do you think of your husband now, woman?' And Dr Gossip supplies her answer: 'I always thought greatly of him, but I think more of him now.' Then Gossip continues: 'I always thought greatly of the Christian faith; but I think more of it now, far more.'[7] Now it seems to me that this is the sort of response Isaiah is fishing for from us – not so much in regard to the Christian faith but of Christ himself. It's as if he wants us to take a hard look at all he tells us of the messianic king in verses 2-5 and then to say,

---

7. See Warren Wiersbe, ed., *Classic Sermons on Suffering* (Grand Rapids: Kregel, 1984), p. 14.

'I always thought greatly of the Lord Jesus Christ, but I think more of him now, far more! How very satisfying he is.'

Thirdly, Isaiah wants to show you **how remarkable God's peace is** (vv. 6-9). And right off Isaiah launches into a *picture* of this peace in verses 6-8. He portrays the kind of conditions one meets under Messiah's rule. It looks like it will involve the removal of the curse on (what we sometimes call) nature. It sort of looks like Paradise regained.

Verses 6-8 are a bit of a shocker to some of us more prosaic souls. But we need to try to get in the mood. Don't start moaning – at least not yet – about whether this picture is literal or figurative. Rather, it's unusual. We know the young lion would ordinarily look at the calf with a glint in his eye and ask, 'Where's the beef?' But not here. We want to scream at the young lad leading that strange herd in verse 6: 'Hey kid, watch out for that leopard behind you!'[8] And won't the ox be prone to say to the lion, 'Hey, this is *my* fodder!'? And the lion replies, 'Would you rather I eat your round steaks then?' Receiving a definite negative, the lion says, 'Okay, then, shut up and share your feed; this is Messiah's kingdom – things are different now.'

After the picture Isaiah gives us the *doctrine* (v. 9) contained in the picture:

> They will not harm or bring ruin
>> in all my holy mountain,
> for the earth shall be filled with knowing Yahweh
>> as the waters cover the sea.

This text doesn't answer all our questions about verses 6-8; in fact, it may raise some issues of its own. But we can say of verse 9: Here's the upshot of the matter; here's the teaching. Note for one thing the *earthiness* of the kingdom here (which shouldn't surprise folks

---

8. 'The predators will so respect the lordship of human beings given to them before the fall (Gen. 1:28) that even the little child will command respect' (Geoffrey Grogan, 'Isaiah,' in *The Expositor's Bible Commentary*, rev. ed., 13 vols. [Grand Rapids: Zondervan, 2008], 6:545).

who pray 'Thy kingdom come' and then immediately add *what that means* in 'thy will be done *on earth*, as it is in heaven'). So don't go wandering off to heaven at this point and try to 'fluffify' Isaiah's picture. Christians may have differing opinions about what 'earth' connotes here: Does it point to a 'millennial' earth (i.e., with an extended reign of the Messiah on earth before the eternal state)? Or is it pointing to the new heavens and new earth (in which case one still has 'earthiness')? The messianic king is not going to give over the earth to the enemy – he is going to put things right in *this place*, in this turf.

I imagine there will be some who will want to dispute with me here (nothing makes Christian folks so touchy as messing with their views of 'last things'), but I hold that it is important to keep the *context*, namely verses 3b-5, in view. The 'And' in verse 6 is significant: 'And the wolf shall stay with the lamb ....' The connectedness of verses 6-8 with verses 3b-5 implies there is a general order, a sequence: The messianic king brings a just regime (vv. 2-5) and then follows a peaceful kingdom (vv. 6-9). The Messiah will impose righteousness, and peace *follows* that. This peace is not something concocted by man – by the UN or by any human scheme. Rather, *victory* brings peace.

And yet Jesus' people know that this peace Isaiah depicts is not completely a 'last thing' thing. Rather Christ's people can have a foretaste of this peace already (see Eph. 2:14-18). In the first-century A.D. the Jews and gentiles didn't belong together – it would be like mixing heifers and bears, wolves and lambs, lions and oxen, toddlers and serpents. You think: No one can bring these together. But Christ does.

Over twenty years ago I recall reading an article in 'Banner of Truth' magazine on 'An Early Communion in New Zealand.' I believe the setting was in the nineteenth century. In any case, there was a remarkable scene as two Maori chiefs approached the Lord's table. One of them, Tamati Wiremu Puna, was trembling. After the service someone asked him about the deep emotion. He explained that the other chief, Panapa, head of another tribe, had in previous years killed and eaten Tamati's father. He added that only the gospel which had given him a new nature could make him eat the same bread and drink the same cup with the murderer of his own father! 'He is our peace' (Eph. 2:14) – even now.

Finally, Isaiah wants you to understand **how unforgotten God's people are** (vv. 10-16). Here we have two footnotes to Isaiah's previous prophecy, one short (v. 10) and one long (vv. 11-16). Both begin with 'And it shall be in that day,' referring to the 'day' of Messiah's kingdom in its fulfillment (a la vv. 1-9). The first footnote has to do with the drawing of the nations (v. 10), the second (vv. 11-16) with the gathering of Israel. Verse 10 depicts how attractive the 'root of Jesse' will prove for the nations – they will come seeking him. It's a picture that fits well with the magnetism the nations will feel for Yahweh's house in 2:2-3. So Christ will have a gentile people who are eager to have Him.

But the second footnote deals with Israel. One wonders why it is so much longer. Perhaps because at this point their situation seemed so utterly hopeless (cf. v. 1, 'the stump of Jesse'), and so the Lord takes special pains to spell out the plans he has for them. Isaiah describes the restoration of Israel under three scenarios:

> (1) Gathering the scattered, vv. 11-12
> (2) Healing the divisions, vv. 13-14
> (3) Removing the obstacles, vv. 15-16

Some notes on the 'footnote'. When verse 11 speaks of a 'second time,' I think the implied 'first time' is the redemption from Egypt in the exodus. But I do not think this (second) gathering refers to the future return from exile in Babylon. That is not 'big' enough. Isaiah ransacks the then-known world to express how extensive this 'gathering' will be – indeed, 'from the four corners of the earth' (v. 12d).[9] It's as if Isaiah wants

9. 'Assyrian kings, including those in the Neo-Assyrian period, regularly designated themselves as "king of the four quarters (of the earth)," that is, of the

to say 'universal'. Then, in verses 13-14, Isaiah sees Israel as a united people in the future, a tenet that is a staple among the prophets (cf., e.g., Jer. 3:18 and Ezek. 37:15-22). And in verses 15-16 Isaiah is saying that there will be absolutely nothing to keep them from coming home – whatever hindrances and barriers there are will be overcome.

At this point I think we need to pay attention to a phrase Isaiah uses twice:

> … the Lord will reach his hand out a second time to acquire
> the remnant of his people (v. 11)
> And there shall be a highway for the remnant of his people
> who remain from Assyria … (v. 16)

'The remnant of his people' – that language reminds us of the message in the name of one of Isaiah's sons, Shear-jashub ('a remnant will return,' see 7:3; 10:20-21). We remember that Isaiah's kids' names were sermons. Someone might try to sympathize and say, 'You poor boy, what a strange name!' But actually he probably didn't mind so much. Shear-jashub would tell you, 'No, it's not so bad – my brother's name is Maher-shalal-hash-baz!' Shear-jashub's name carried a double message: (1) a remnant will return, and (2) only a remnant will return. Certainty and restriction. Sometimes one meets such two-edged statements.

I recall the first time we lived in Mississippi. We had begun to do some work on the outside of our house, something like cleaning up and painting the trim. And while we were working, Eva, our nice, Baptist, next-door neighbor came out and exclaimed, 'Looks like you folks are really getting with it!' One's first impulse is to take that as a compliment about one's industry. But was it? There may be a subtle undertone there, as if to say, 'Well, you haven't been getting with it up to this point but, at last, apparently you are.' It may be a compliment – or a criticism.

---

entire inhabited world' (David W. Baker, *Isaiah*, Zondervan Illustrated Bible Background Commentary [Grand Rapids: Zondervan, 2009/2013], p. 64).

Something like that seems implied in the 'remnant' note here. A remnant will be gathered and brought home against all hazards, but this will be (only) a *remnant* of his people. 'Not all who are descended from Israel belong to Israel' (Rom. 9:6).

Nevertheless, with this proviso Yahweh primarily intends to *assure* his people. No matter where they are, Yahweh knows where his elect people are. He knows his remnant and will bring them back. No place can hide them, no obstacle prevent them, no circumstance blot them from his view. Yahweh does not cast off his remnant from national Israel.[10] They are not lost to him; he doesn't 'lose track' of his people (cf. Isa. 49:14-16a). Shepherds that tells stories of having ninety-nine sheep and missing *one* and going after that one can be depended upon to know where you are.

Donald Grey Barnhouse told of several oak trees he once planted by his house. All but one grew more than twenty feet high. That particular one was damaged and died at the soil line. But the root system was intact and a shoot came up, quite spindly and weak. Barnhouse was going to tear it out and put in a new tree, but a horticulturist told him that that shoot would catch up with the other trees. This stretched Barnhouse's arboreal faith, but he left it alone. After two years, it was six feet high; after four years, more than twelve feet. It had a fine branch system.[11] So don't be in despair over the 'dead' look of things; don't be put off by the stump (v. 1); there are times when God's kingdom looks like it's whacked down to nothing. But the shoot of Jesse will thrive.

---

10. Note Oswalt, p. 286: 'Certainly, believers were gathered to the Messiah from every part of the world, and v. 10, in a fashion reminiscent of 2:2-4, seems to begin the section with a reference to the nations at large. Nevertheless, the primary focus of the passage seems to be upon the historical nation of Israel, so that one is led to believe it points to some great final ingathering of the Jewish people such as that referred to by Paul in Romans 11.'

11. Donald Grey Barnhouse, *Let Me Illustrate* (Westwood, NJ: Revell, 1967), p. 177.

8 WHAT THEN SHALL WE SAY TO THESE THINGS?
(Isaiah 12)

(1)   And you shall say on that day:
       'I will give you thanks, Yahweh,
       for you have been angry with me;
       let your anger turn away
       that you may comfort me.

(2)   See! God (is) my salvation!
       I will trust and not feel dread,
       for Yah Yahweh is my strength and my song
       and he has become my salvation.'

(3)   And you shall draw water joyfully
              from the springs of salvation.

(4)   And you shall say on that day:
       'Give thanks to Yahweh,

call on his name,
make known among the peoples his deeds,
proclaim that his name is lifted high!

(5)   Sing praises to Yahweh,
for he has acted majestically;
let this be made known in all the earth.'

(6)   Cry out and shout for joy, resident of Zion,
for great in your midst is the Holy One of Israel.

Some people are known for their reserved, unflappable, un-excitable demeanor. Former president Calvin Coolidge was notorious for such both in legend and fact. Once while Vice President he was presiding when a cornerstone was laid at a public building. Coolidge turned the obligatory spadeful of dirt, and workmen laid the stone. The crowd expected some remarks but none came. Finally, the master of ceremonies asked for a few words from the Vice President. Coolidge pondered a moment, then pointed to his spadeful of dirt, and observed: 'There's a – mighty fine fishworm.' And walked off to his limo. He was so low-key that when news came that he was dead, a woman journalist jibed, 'How can they tell?'[1]

Isaiah 12, however, is anything but a 'Coolidge text'. Isaiah 12 stands in front of us, stretches out its hands, and shouts, 'What then shall we say to these things?'[2] Once more the tiny initial conjunction ('And') implies that chapter 12 simply flows on from what has preceded; and the references to 'in that day' in verses 1 and 4 immediately call to mind the same phrase in

1. Paul F. Boller, Jr., *Presidential Anecdotes* (New York: Penguin, 1981), pp. 235, 240.

2. Ray Ortlund uses the Romans 8:31 rubric to introduce his treatment of Isaiah 12 as well. I'd gladly acknowledge my indebtedness to him except the Romans 8:31 link was in my lecture notes before his book came out. His introductory comments to ch. 12 are superb; cf. *Isaiah: God Saves Sinners* (Wheaton, IL: Crossway, 2005), pp. 119-20.

11:10 and 11 and so alert us that chapter 12 celebrates that final establishment of Messiah's kingdom that chapter 11 describes.

Before our exposition it will be well to map out the structure of the chapter, for it is very carefully put together. I agree with John L. MacKay that there are two songs (vv. 1-2 and vv. 4-5) and each one is followed by a prophetic 'comment' (vv. 3 and 6).[3] In a bit more detail it looks like this:

Verses 1-2
>V. 1a: 'And you [singular] shall say on that day ... ,'
>followed by 1st person singular expression of praise

>Verse 3
>>2nd person plural prediction of action
>>Keynote: joy

Verses 4-5
>V. 4a: 'And you [plural] shall say on that day ... ,'
>followed by 2nd person plural call to praise

>Verse 6
>>2nd feminine singular imperative command
>>to Lady Zion
>>Keynote: joy

Now let us go inside the packaging and discover what the redeemed are singing about. And they speak of **the one miracle we need** as the premier item for thanksgiving (v. 1). The text seems to be both praise ('I will give thanks, Yahweh, for you have been angry with me') and yet partly prayer ('let your anger turn away that you may comfort me'). This request-mode ('let your anger turn away') in the second half of the verse is the better way to take the Hebrew, though English versions will make it sound more definite (e.g., NIV).[4] So the worshiper both

---

3. See *A Study Commentary on Isaiah,* 2 vols. (Darlington: Evangelical Press, 2008), 1:307.

4. See Gary V. Smith, *Isaiah 1-39,* New American Commentary (Nashville:

admits he has been under God's anger and asks that he may be relieved of it. Yet the request-form of the last two lines does not suggest uncertainty but anticipation. Here is the supreme need. Here is the one matter above all matters that must be resolved. One can face it in corporate terms, as in 1:4:

> Ugh! A nation that keeps sinning,
>> a people loaded down with guilt,
>> a seed of evil-doers,
>> sons acting corruptly!
> They have abandoned Yahweh;
>> they have scorned the Holy One of Israel;
>> they are nothing but strangers.

Or in personal terms, as in 6:5:

> Woe to me!
> For I am destroyed!
> For I am a man of unclean lips,
> and I dwell in the midst of a people of unclean lips … .

But there is no song to sing unless God's wrath is faced; unless my theology and faith can somehow negotiate God's wrath, there can be no deep and exuberant joy.

I have never been able to forget (and I know I have referred to it before) an article Paul Cook wrote for the 'Banner of Truth' magazine some years ago. He told of missing a train connection and speaking with another fellow as he waited for the next train. This man had flown for the RAF in World War II, told of bombing missions over Germany, and averred that in spite of propaganda to the contrary, they *had* bombed civilian populations, including hapless women and children. The memories, the faces, the horrors still plagued him. In a pitiful atonement gesture he regularly handed out sweets to kids in care homes.

Broadman & Holman, 2007), 282; and Alec Motyer, *The Prophecy of Isaiah* (Downers Grove, IL: Inter-Varsity, 1993), p. 128.

He recalled going round some of London's churches after the war, hoping he might hear something to address his guilt. His summary was that the preaching he heard was 'a lot of drivel about the love of God'. That brutal, seemingly irreverent comment touches the nerve of the matter. Odd as it seems, what he seemed to long for was to hear of the *wrath* of God, for someone to speak to him of the anger of God and then what might be done about it. But it wasn't touched.

It's what the tax collector in Jesus' story craved (see Luke 18:9-14). Strictly speaking, he did not pray for God to 'be merciful to me, the sinner.' The verb is *hilaskomai* – it presupposes the sacrifice being made there in the temple for the people's sins and so really should be translated, 'Make an atonement for me, a sinner!'[5] But the verb points to an atoning sacrifice that is a means of turning aside divine wrath – and so HCSB translates verse 13, 'God, turn your wrath from me – a sinner!' We know that Jesus himself is that sort of provision (1 John 2:2). 'Let your anger turn away' – that is the miracle above all miracles that we need. Those five words express what is both utterly outlandish and absolutely necessary.

Secondly, the redeemed celebrate **the only security we have** (v. 2). And it's easy to ignore the wonder of this. So Gary Smith reminds us that the verse begins with that Hebrew particle *hinnēh* (hin-nay) that always suggests some degree of wonder or surprise, as if to say at this point: 'Look, can you believe this?!'[6] Of all things, God is my salvation – and so I can rest in that.

---

5. See discussion in Kenneth E. Bailey, *Poet and Peasant* and *Through Peasant Eyes* (combined ed.; Grand Rapids: Eerdmans, 1983), p. 154.

6. Smith, 282. There may be variations in the degree of surprise conveyed by *hinnēh*. In Genesis 29:25 it packs a severe jolt. Laban has tricked Jacob in the wife deal and when the latter wakes up in the morning, 'Behold! It was Leah!' Maybe a better idiomatic translation would be, 'Oh no! It was Leah!' I'm not demeaning Leah but only trying to express Jacob's shock. Sometimes a standard and staid rendering like 'Behold' can keep us from feeling the punch in a text.

And that's exactly what he does. If 'God is my salvation,' then he can go on to say, 'I will trust and not feel dread.' Then the rest of the verse implies that he says that '*for* [note the reasoning] Yah Yahweh is my strength and my song and he has become my salvation.' So what comes before and after gives him the basis for saying, 'I will trust and not feel dread.'[7]

That statement is no stale sentiment of pious trivia. One must remember the whole muddle of the historical context. Here are people who faced the Syro-Ephraimite threat in chapter 7, who would be nearly strangled by the near-omnipotence of Assyria, and yet who are promised that the stump of Jesse will become a kingdom of righteousness and peace into which they will surely be gathered.In light of that, in view of the abrasions and disasters they will endure, it is no light matter to say, 'I will trust and not feel dread.' But they have a God who is not only 'salvation' and 'song', but especially 'my strength' – the One who fortifies and toughens and braces and heartens and supports in the thick of it all.

Just days ago I was re-reading some of Don McClure's missionary reports. He was a Presbyterian pioneer missionary and in the 1950s was serving among the Anuaks in Pokwo, Ethiopia. He told of how different the Anuak Christians were from others in their tribe who were forever resorting to the witchdoctors. He told of one of his Anuak Christians whose son was fishing and was bitten by a very poisonous puff adder. The father calmly brought the boy to McClure to treat. He said, 'If the medicine will not help him, then our prayers will. And if he dies, our lives are in God's hands.' McClure said the lad was going to recover. But he also teased the father with: 'Why didn't you kill a sheep and pour the blood on your son as you

---

7. John Oswalt says that this 'is what Isaiah was attempting to get Ahaz to say in 7:2-9' (*The Book of Isaiah: Chapters 1-39*, New International Commentary on the Old Testament [Grand Rapids: Eerdmans, 1986], p. 293).

would have done three years ago?' The man raised his hands above his head in horror. 'That was,' he said, 'in other days. Now we believe only in the blood of Jesus.'[8] Eighth-century Judah may seem far removed from twentieth century Ethiopia and a Judean believer from a not-so-long-ago converted African tribesman. But those words – 'if the medicine will not help him, then our prayers will. And if he dies, we are in God's hands' – those words are simply another way of saying, 'I will trust and not feel dread.'

'And you shall draw water joyfully from the springs of salvation.' Here at verse 3 the grammatical pattern changes: the 'you' is plural and the second-person address indicates it's the prophet's comment as a kind of footnote to what has preceded. We could say verse 3 highlights **the sure assurance we hear**. But what does all this water-drawing have to do with assurance?

It may help to realize that this song seems to have another patch of Scripture in mind. The last half of verse 2 is almost an exact quote from Exodus 15:2: 'Yah is my strength and (my) song, and he has become my salvation.'[9] That was Moses and Israel's song of celebration over Yahweh's decimating of the Egyptian army. But if we recall chapter 11, we note that there are also Egyptian 'memories' there; e.g., in 11:11 (the 'second time' implying a 'first time' when Yahweh gathered his people from Egypt) and in 11:15-16 (there was a 'highway' for Israel when they exited Egypt before). So it seems that the Exodus story is the memory backdrop for Isaiah 11–12. We should then look at verse 3 in that light. Of course, the imagery of verse 3 could be general and non-specific, but, fact is, we do

8. Charles Partee, *Adventure in Africa: The Story of Don McClure* (Grand Rapids: Zondervan, 1990), p. 282.

9. Yah seems to be an abbreviated form of Yahweh. Both names are used in 12:2, just Yah in Exodus 15:2.

recall some noteworthy 'water' stories in post-Exodus time. There was Marah (Exod. 15:22-26), so disappointing with its necessary but undrinkable water – until Yahweh 'healed' it. There was Elim (Exod. 15:27), a delightful oasis, with its 'twelve springs of water and seventy palm trees'. Then there was Rephidim (Exod. 17:1-7), where Yahweh told Moses to strike the rock – out gushed water. These episodes were meant to teach Israel that the God who can deliver from Egypt will surely sustain in the wilderness. The God who saves can also be trusted to satisfy. 'The God who saves continues to minister salvation to his people as an ever available reality to enjoy.'[10] The experience of salvation never 'dries up'. The God who saves also supplies. There is refreshment along the way.

I still remember how delighted I was when I first read through Bunyan's *Pilgrim's Progress* and came to his description of Christian at the base of the Hill Difficulty. There was a spring at the base of the hill and Christian drank. But then it became arduous:

> I looked then after Christian, to see him go up the hill, when I perceived he fell from running to going, and from going to clambering upon his hands and his knees, because of the steepness of the place. Now about midway to the top of the hill was a pleasant arbour, made by the Lord of the hill, for the refreshment of weary travellers.

A pleasant arbour, 'made by the Lord of the hill.' Is that not a Yahweh-touch? The Lord who saves also sustains, the one who rescues also refreshes. Wasn't this the same assurance Isaiah used when seeking to bolster up future exiles who would return to Israel? Think of the dangers and the needs and the problems and the unknowns. And Isaiah takes them back to the wilderness, to the water-supplying God:

---

10. Motyer, p. 129.

> They did not thirst when he led them
> > through the deserts;
> he made water flow for them from the rock;
> he split the rock and the water gushed out
> > (Isa. 48:21, ESV).

Naturally, 12:3 seems to refer to the satisfaction and joy of Yahweh's people 'on that day' when Messiah visibly and openly reigns. And yet there seems to be a sense that this is also true 'on the way' to that kingdom. Yahweh has a way of arranging for 'springs of salvation' to show up in the most desolate premises.[11]

Fourthly, this song speaks of **the clear testimony we bear** (vv. 4-5). Verse 4 begins with another 'You shall say on that day.' The 'you' here is plural, referring to the whole community of Yahweh's worshipers. In these verses, Yahweh's people seem to declare their mission. When they say, 'Give thanks to Yahweh, call on his name' (v. 4b) I assume they are speaking to themselves of their own obligation to thank and worship Yahweh. But then in verses 4c-5 their testimony takes an 'outward' turn. This testimony 'among the peoples' could simply be declarative (as if putting on public record Yahweh's saving deeds), but, taking into account other Isaiah texts (see below), one suspects this testimony is also invitational.

My wife is from western Kansas and still receives her home-town newspaper (now a weekly) in the mail. Not long ago there was a reprint of a previously published column about what was going on in her town back in 1913. I was amused to read that a new game called 'Christianity' was being played in certain parts of town: the girls get on one side and are the Christians, and the boys get on the other side and are the heathen. Then

---

11. All of 12:1-3 is a superb summary of kingdom bounties, showing that Yahweh's people are secure from wrath (v. 1), fear (v. 2), and need (v. 3). cf. MacKay, 1:308.

the heathen 'embrace' Christianity. Well, that seems a little too easy, though a good excuse I suppose for hugging your favorite female. But gag that it was, in its own contorted way it testifies to a quality of biblical faith – it always looks outward and wants to draw the 'heathen' in.

And so here Yahweh's people speak of their witness among 'outsiders':

> [M]ake known among the peoples his deeds,
> proclaim that his name is lifted high!
> Sing praises to Yahweh,
> for he has acted majestically;
> let this be made known in all the earth (vv. 4c-5).

Their testimony is to be carried out 'among the peoples' (gentiles) and to be 'known in all the earth' and not merely in Israel.

Note *what* is to be made known: Yahweh's deeds (v. 4c) and 'how he has acted' (v. 5). God's people are to declare Yahweh's objective deeds, not their own subjective experiences. They don't dwell on how they feel but on what God has done. That would take in the saving deeds Yahweh has done in calling and gathering and delivering and preserving a people for himself – that is, the whole thrilling record of redemptive history to date. And in our own time we could include more of God's 'acting majestically,' especially his Son's wrath-absorbing death (Mark 15:34), his death-defying resurrection (2 Tim. 1:10), terror-excluding dominion (Eph. 1:20-22), and justice-imposing coming (2 Thess. 1:6-8).

But back to Isaiah 12 – and beyond! We meet this theme of testimony to, or the 'coming' of, the nations throughout Isaiah. We have just read of it in 11:10-12, where the messianic 'root of Jesse' who will bring his glorious reign on earth (11:1-9) will also be 'a banner to the peoples' and will be 'the one the nations will come seeking' (11:10). The Lord will bring such a full salvation for he will both 'raise a banner for the *nations*' and 'gather the outcasts of *Israel*' (11:12, emphasis mine). Gary Smith cites a number of Isaiah texts (in addition to 11:10-12) which speak of the nations knowing about Yahweh and coming to worship him (2:2-4; 19:19-25; 45:22-25; 60:1-9; 66:19-21).[12] And sometimes, it seems, the testimony of believing Israel plays a part in the 'coming' of the gentiles/nations (note 2:3b in context and 66:19-20, though some would construe the latter passage differently).[13]

Whether 'on that day' or along the way to that day Jesus always seems to have 'other sheep' (John 10:16) he is eager to gather, and somehow he seems to prefer to use the testimony of his people in order to gather them. And even if this testimony 'among the peoples' is not always spectacular, it is nevertheless telling. Recently I was reading the newsletter of an international mission agency. Their workers have labored for a number of years in a particular country, one they could not name for security reasons. There a group of Muslim community leaders came to the mission team and said, 'We have been watching you for several years, and have seen how you have really helped our people and that you can be trusted. We want you to tell us about your Christian faith.' 'He is the one the nations will come seeking' (11:10).

Finally, Isaiah wants us to see **the high privilege we enjoy** (v. 6). Here again, in my view, as in verse 3, the prophet turns aside to instruct or comment. And here he tells Lady Zion she should simply be beside herself with joy.[14] What is it that

---

12. Smith, p. 283.

13. I think that in Romans 15:16 Paul may well be looking at his ministry through the lens of Isaiah 66:19-20. He may even be viewing himself as one of the (Israelite?) 'survivors' (Isa. 66:19; note Paul's identity as an unrejected Israelite, part of the remnant chosen by grace, Rom. 11:1, 5), who declares Yahweh's glory among the nations and so brings many gentile 'brothers' to be a part of the 'Jerusalem' people.

14. Derek Thomas nicely highlights the responses expected of God's people in Isaiah 12: trust (2a), thanks (4), and joy (3, 6) (*God Delivers: Isaiah Simply Explained* [Darlington: Evangelical Press, 1991], pp. 117-19).

thrills her, that goads her to shouts of joy? The residence of the Holy One of Israel in her midst (v. 6b).

One can hardly help but think of the Book of Exodus again and of the climactic text of that book: 'And they shall make for me a sanctuary, and I shall dwell in their midst' (Exod. 25:8). That, in one sense, is the ultimate. So the high point of Exodus is not escape from Egypt or covenant at Sinai but God's tent among Israel's tents. Not the sea or the mountain but the tent. Yahweh simply can't get close enough to his people – he is obsessed with dwelling among them. And that ought to thrill the socks off of his people. That is what we find here: 'Cry out and shout for joy … for great in your midst is the Holy One of Israel.'

Isaiah is very fond of calling Yahweh 'the Holy One of Israel' (twenty-six times in the book). And, as van Imschoot explains, the expression

> contains a paradox: Yahweh is distinct from every creature inasmuch as he is holy. Yet if he is bound to Israel inasmuch as he is 'the Holy One of Israel,' it is because he established a relation which has for its goal the sanctification of Israel.[15]

The phrase almost contains an insoluble conundrum: Yahweh is the Holy One and yet the Holy One *of Israel*. How can he remain the Holy One and yet stand in relation to Israel? How can he be holy yet dwell in the midst of a people of unclean lips (6:5)? (Chapter 6 points to an answer). 'Holy One' makes sense; one almost chokes, however, to say 'Holy One *of Israel*.' But the Holy One of Israel has plans to make Israel partakers of his holiness (4:3-4) and that will change everything.

In the meantime our text implies that the kingdom blessing that should produce the deepest joy and quickest goose-

---

15. Paul van Imschoot, *Theology of the Old Testament—Vol. I: God* (Tournai: Desclee, 1954), 48. Geoffrey Grogan picks up the paradox by noting that 'he is distinct [Holy One] but not aloof [of Israel]' ('Isaiah,' in *The Expositor's Bible Commentary*, rev. ed., 13 vols. [Grand Rapids: Zondervan, 2008], 6:551).

bumps for Yahweh's people is his very presence in their midst. Surely this ought to be our attitude even in these on-the-way days to Isaiah-12-time. I myself do not consciously think of this privilege as I should. Perhaps it takes someone who seems more of a stranger to such matters to teach us. I think of that woman in Aberavon (Wales), where Martyn Lloyd-Jones was serving in his first pastorate. She was a spirit-medium and collected a good fee for leading a spiritist meeting on Sunday evenings. But one Sunday night she was ill, couldn't go out to the rendezvous, and couldn't help but notice the numbers of folks passing her house on the way to the chapel. They seemed to have a sort of 'anticipation' written on them and she therefore determined to attend a service herself. Well, she did that – and came to Christ, and walked on in a consistent life. What is so fascinating, however, was part of her testimony:

> The moment I entered your chapel and sat down on a seat amongst the people, I was conscious of a supernatural power. I was conscious of the same sort of supernatural power as I was accustomed to in our spiritist meetings, but there was one big difference: I had the feeling that the power in your chapel was a *clean* power.[16]

'I was conscious of a supernatural power – a clean power.' Would that I had more of a 'feeling-ness' of the triune God's presence among his people. By that I don't mean having some soggy emotional sensation but a far more distinct realization that the Holy One of Israel himself is, once more, there, among his 'Israel'. It brings on the same wonder and thrill as when one reads, 'This man welcomes sinners and eats with them' (Luke 15:2). Sometimes the Pharisees got it right.

---

16. Iain H. Murray, *David Martyn Lloyd-Jones: The First Forty Years 1899-1939* (Edinburgh: Banner of Truth, 1982), p. 221.

Christian Focus Publications

Our mission statement –

STAYING FAITHFUL

In dependence upon God we seek to impact the world through literature faithful to His infallible Word, the Bible. Our aim is to ensure that the Lord Jesus Christ is presented as the only hope to obtain forgiveness of sin, live a useful life and look forward to heaven with Him.

Our books are published in four imprints:

CHRISTIAN
FOCUS

Popular works including biographies, commentaries, basic doc-trine and Christian living.

CHRISTIAN
HERITAGE

Books representing some of the best material from the rich heritage of the church.

MENTOR

Books written at a level suitable for Bible College and seminary students, pastors, and other serious readers. The imprint includes commentaries, doctrinal studies, examination of current issues and church history.

CF4•K

Children's books for quality Bible teaching and for all age groups: Sunday school curriculum, puzzle and activity books; personal and family devotional titles, biographies and inspirational stories – because you are never too young to know Jesus!

Christian Focus Publications Ltd,
Geanies House, Fearn, Ross-shire,
IV20 1TW, Scotland, United Kingdom.
www.christianfocus.com